The Life of the Law

The Life of the Law

Anthropological Projects

Laura Nader

UNIVERSITY OF CALIFORNIA PRESS

Berkeley   Los Angeles   London

University of California Press
Berkeley and Los Angeles, California

University of California Press, Ltd.
London, England

© 2002 by the Regents of the University of California
First paperback printing 2005

Library of Congress Cataloging-in-Publication Data

Nader, Laura.
   The life of the law : anthropological projects / Laura Nader.
      p.   cm.
   Includes bibliographical references and index.
   ISBN 978-0-520-23163-4 (pbk : alk. paper)
      1. Law and anthropology.   I. Title.
K487.A57 N33   2002
340'.115—dc21   2001027675

Manufactured in the United States of America
10   09   08   07   06   05   04   03   02   01
10   9   8   7   6   5   4   3   2   1

The paper used in this publication meets the minimum
requirements of ANSI/NISO Z39.48–1992 (R 1997) (*Permanence
of Paper*).

In memory of my grandson Nels

CONTENTS

ACKNOWLEDGMENTS

First and foremost, I am grateful for the invitation from the Department of Legal Sciences of the University of Trento, Italy, to deliver the 1996 Cardozo Lectures. Professor Diego Quaglioni, director of the law school, was my host during the lecture period from May 24 to May 25, and he brought together a most inspiring community of colleagues to participate in the events accompanying the lectures. Among them was Professor Rodolfo Sacco—clearly the most inspirational of leaders in scholarship on law in culture and society for a younger generation of Italian legal scholars. I am especially appreciative of the warm hospitality, the good companionship and wonderful conversations, and the food and drink that I shared with my hosts, Ugo Mattei and Elizabetta Grande. The combination of playfulness and serious talk, concern and responsibility, laughter and observation was memorable. And I thank Ugo Mattei especially for being so adept at cutting bureaucratic tape and, later, for quickly putting into practice his newly acquired awareness of what it means to be coercively harmonized.

The process of preparing the lectures for publication was interrupted by academic and personal trials and tribulations. There was no financial support to free me from teaching and university responsibilities either before or after the lectures, and the longer I waited to get back to the lectures, the more I thought I needed to entirely rewrite them. In the final analysis, I resisted the urge to rewrite and decided to publish the lectures in Italian as they were originally prepared with attention in the revision to clarifying the issues therein. In preparing revisions for publication in English, I was especially challenged by my anonymous reviewers, one of whom wanted, first and foremost, a book about the relationship between litigation and social change in contemporary democracies in the context of knowledge exchange between legal activists and academic anthropologists, both of whom have much to teach each other. I see my contribution as but a start in such directions.

In writing these lectures, I have benefited immeasurably from the work of others in and out of anthropology, particularly the anthropological work that we call ethnography. In addition, I drew on my own field experiences over the past forty years in Mexico among the Zapotec, in Lebanon among the Shia Muslims in the south, in the United States among consumers of products and services, and in Morocco among the common folk in courts during Ramadan. The students who worked with me on the anthropology of law, from Berkeley and elsewhere, both graduate and undergraduate, carried out firsthand fieldwork, which resulted in ethnographic works that I edited and published with them: *The Disputing Process* (1978, with my graduate students working in the Berkeley Village Law Project), *No Access to Law* (1980, with undergraduates working on the Berkeley Complaint Project), and *Essays on Controlling Processes* (1994 and 1996, jointly with undergraduates and graduates). Finally, I am fortunate to have participated in the many high-level public debates in judicial councils, at American Bar Association meetings, and among law and development policymakers and law school colleagues, about the place of law in the United States and elsewhere from the early 1960s to the present.

Since the late 1950s, funding for my work on law has come from Harvard University, where I was a graduate student; from the Mexican government, in support of my first fieldwork in Oaxaca; from the Carnegie Corporation to study how Americans complain; from the Wenner-Gren Foundation to assess the findings published in *The Disputing Process;* and from the University of California at Berkeley and Los Angeles to support fieldwork in southern Lebanon (1961) and exploratory work in Morocco (1980). Support for writing and thinking about these issues came from the Center for Advanced Study in the Behavioral Sciences at Stanford, California, from 1963 to 1964 and the Woodrow Wilson International Center for Scholars at the Smithsonian Institution, Washington, D.C., from 1979 to 1980. Intellectual exchange with law school colleagues was plentiful during my teaching semesters at Yale Law School (1971), Harvard Law School (1983–1984), and Stanford Law School for several consecutive years in the 1990s. The Center for Advanced Study in the Behavioral Sciences and the Institute of International Studies at the University of California, Berkeley, supported the filming and production of my first documentary film, *To Make the Balance* (1966), and PBS supported the Odyssey Project, which resulted in *Little Injustices,* a documentary film comparing Zapotec and U.S. practices in dispute management (1984).

I am thankful to my family, especially my father and mother, for being my best teachers; to my colleagues Elizabeth Colson, Ellen Hertz, Roberto Gonzalez, Tarek Milleron, Claire Nader, and Linda Coco for careful reading and critical commentary on parts of the manuscript, and especially to Elizabeth Colson for sage advice and pithy comments; and to Paul Bohannan, Jenny Beer, June Starr, Michael J. Lowy, JoAnn Martin, Barbara Yngvesson, Sally Merry, David Trubek, Andrew Gunder Frank, Boaventura de Sousa Santos, Annelise Riles, Eve Darian-Smith, Beth Mertz, John Borneman, and many others for talks about law and society and antidisciplinary issues more generally. Thanks are also due to Jay Ou, Laura Bathurst, Patricia Marquez, Patricia Urteaga-Crovetto, and Sue Wilson for library research and critical thoughts, and to my constructive and anonymous reviewers for expecting more. To Jim Clark of the University of California Press, I extend many thanks for his longtime encouragement and support. Our incredibly agile Berkeley anthropology librarian, Suzanne Calpestri, was ever ready to help as only one who is interested in the substance can. Holly Halligan was supportive and intelligent in her typing of the manuscript (and worth more than her weight in gold), as was Liza Grandia, with her lively eye and mind that saved the day when the day needed saving. Shirley Taylor gave editorial help and substantive suggestions with competence and good cheer. The final manuscript was edited with care by Carlotta Shearson and Erika Büky for the benefit of the intelligent general reader. Responsibility for the finished product is, alas, mine.

Berkeley, California
August 15, 2000

Introduction

In the 1960s the possibility of anthropologists teaching in law schools would have been anathema in most law school faculties. In fact, the relationships between anthropologists and lawyers might have been antagonistic. "How dare you speak about the law when you are not a lawyer?" was the first greeting I received at an interdisciplinary symposium. There has been a crossing of the Rubicon; disciplines are blurring. Not long ago only the few were interested in anthropologists' esoteric works on African customary law. Today those interested in traditional peacemaking in Africa include professionals from disparate fields—psychology, law, political science, globalization studies, and military studies, as well as the study of pan-African nationalism. Not so long ago those who studied court decisions spoke about *judicial* decision-making, as if plaintiffs and defendants and their respective lawyers were of no consequence to legal decision-making. Not so long ago, in the 1960s, ethnographic research was the province of the anthropologist, and

I

culture was our core concept. Today concepts of culture are loose on the streets as well as in the academy, where we have cultural law, cultural psychology, cultural sociology, and cultural studies. There is some convergence among those who study culture, but in retrospect, theoretical and ethnographic breakthroughs in anthropology are often treated casually in the move across disciplinary lines. Not so paradigmatic shifts: anthropology as the study of "us" as exotic other is here to stay.

In this book, the civil plaintiff, whose connections with daily life are filtered by controlling ideologies and legal discourse, cautions us about where the law is heading, where it should lead, and why. If indeed the legal power of the individual is eroding in favor of the power of the state and the corporation, then a look down the road is in order.

Writing this book provided me with the occasion to clarify my thinking about the anthropology of law. First, it gave me the opportunity to articulate for myself the working relations between lawyers and anthropologists, as well as between anthropologists and other social scientists. It was an opportunity to assess the worth of the interdisciplinary efforts of the past forty years against a backdrop of nineteenth-century scholarship that was somewhat less constrained and often more worldly. Second, it was a way of assessing contributions to the understanding of what in recent human history we call law, a way of gauging the contemporary value of twentieth-century anthropological studies of law in small communities. And last, the book forced me to contemplate, more or less autobiographically, my train of thought about the plaintiff—only some of which appears in the pages to follow—in my four decades of research on the anthropology of law *in* context. During these decades, the environment of legal imperialism has changed from European legal models implanted in distant colonies in the Arab world, in Africa, and across the Pacific and Southeast Asia, to increasingly large-scale concentrations of global power and a new world order that is, at bottom, an Americanization of the laws of other peoples and nations almost everywhere.

My anthropological work coincided with special junctures in world events. As a young anthropologist, I worked in small Zapotec mountain communities in the Rincón area of the Sierra Madre of Oaxaca, Mexico. The communities were mostly self-sufficient and isolated from city life; residents traveled by foot or on beasts of burden. When I arrived in the field in 1957, large-scale development projects were viewed positively, and the imminent arrival of a road into the Rincón Zapotec area was taken by many there as a sign of hope. These Sierra villages have rich natural resources. Some have extensive timber. The soil is rich, and the abandoned mines are indicative of past and probable future mineral exploitation. At the time of my early fieldwork as a young professor at the University of California, Berkeley, I was simultaneously living through the Free Speech movement and the anti–Vietnam War movement, and like others was affected by the Cold War and the many rights movements of the 1960s, all the more so because my teaching responsibilities revolved around law, social control, social order, and warfare.

When I recall that early period, I am dismayed, not nostalgic, for even then I could see where the Zapotec were headed. The transformations I sadly projected for the Zapotec communities have occurred and indeed accelerated since the end of the Cold War: out-migration, community destabilization, the appearance of poverty (in a mineral-rich and ecologically diverse area), increases in the incidence of AIDS and tuberculosis, the erosion of autonomy, poor sanitary conditions, the increasing presence of multinational interests and consumer desire, and by 1997 the ubiquitous presence of the Mexican military.

During a 1994 visit to Mexico, I was interested to read an abridged version of a Lloyd's report (1993) on economic possibilities in Mexico. This four-page report, which I found in my hotel room, mentioned a new law "which eliminates fifteen former requirements for federal approval of foreign investments and permits new projects within the country without federal authorization." Areas of foreign investment mentioned included mining, timber, oil, and agricultural enterprises. I asked myself Where are these plentiful resources relative to Indian lands? If they are on Indian lands, why did the government and others, including anthropologists, refer to the Indian peoples of Mexico as poor? When Mexican government documents refer to reform with emphasis on individual private ownership of lands, does the government, as part of its divestment plans, intend to transfer land from communal to private ownership, say to new investment companies? What can indigenous law possibly do under such conditions of power disparity?

But since I posed these questions, times have changed not only in Mexico but also in the United States. We are still living through the Reagan revolution of the 1980s (and the continuation of that revolution under President George Bush, President Clinton, and now George W. Bush), which targets the progressive accomplishments of the 1960s and the New Deal before that. Part of what was (and is) targeted for restriction was access to justice that had been opened up by the Civil Rights

Acts and federal legal-aid programs. Access to justice had been a burning issue that fueled the original American Revolution. The reactionary move to restrict access to justice has not yet peaked, especially in the area of tort law. While the United States works to spread democracy abroad, trade agreements like the North American Free Trade Agreement (NAFTA) and the General Agreement on Tariffs and Trade (GATT) challenge the sovereignty of national law; globalization spearheaded by many American transnational corporations is causing increasing mischief, still justified under the banner of trade and development by means of law. These changes made me sit up and take notice.

The object of my study gradually moved from overt social control, as found in disputing forums, to cultural control or mind colonization, an arena that incorporates law but goes beyond law to permeate everyday life. By the 1980s, I was working both abroad and at home and was able to see a union of my research interests in the little village democracies in Mexico where I started my work, in the country of which I am a citizen, and in the world in which we all live. These sites, which I traverse in chapter 1, are linked in my work by the connections between litigation and social change in contemporary democracies, both local and national. Plaintiffs and defendants and their purposes have changed in the world where increasing numbers of poor people are affected by a climate in which everything is for sale. Body parts are trafficking from the south to the north, and within leading industrial countries as well. Social distinctions are increasingly the basis for life-and-death decisions—literally, in the case of the death penalty. The difference between "them" and "us" is being erased, since environmental pollution and infectious diseases know no borders. We now all live in a kind of Third World, a world where freely shared knowledge is fast becoming an endangered species, owing to patent developments and intellectual property law, a world where class disparities are salient. At the same time, the practices of law are shrinking from the larger purposes without which law has no legitimacy. Our scholarship is, I believe, increasingly commensurate with the corporatization of universities, not just in the United States but worldwide. This is a time when big business is in everybody's business, a time when self-censorship is becoming ingrained, a development that encourages potential critical thinkers to move away from the concrete toward the abstract. Injustice, however, is not abstract. Law cases brought by plaintiffs are not abstract, nor is the regulation of such cases abstract.

I originally chose *The Life of the Law: Anthropological Projects* as the title of this book because "the life of the law" was the topic of a lecture I gave in Trento, Italy; the audience was composed primarily of lawyers and judges who wished to know more about anthropological interest in their subject matter. The topic allowed me freedom to connect a number of issues that have interested me while studying law in context and the plaintiff's role in disputing, issues such as power, control, autonomy, colonialism, industrialization, and the imposition of Western law. Some of my colleagues and acquaintances have wondered about my continuing fascination with dispute processes. To them I say that the present academic scene is cursed by trendiness. Sticking with a subject like disputing, whether trendy or not, in a world that is changing at every level—the small village, the nation, the globe, a world without government—has led me to think even more intensely about what ordinary people think is important: disputes. Disputes under changing conditions have challenged anthropologists to rethink methodologies and old theories, to rethink the place of our work in history, and to think about the work of our colleagues in allied areas from other disciplinary points of view. We owe it to ourselves and to those we study to recognize the creative thrust of the plaintiff because of a political blindness associated with the assumption that the content of law originates with powerful groups and flows down to the powerless (Dwyer 1979). Relatively less powerful plaintiffs have been known to challenge the assumption that law originates only with the powerful.

In my first article on the subject, "The Anthropological Study of Law," I began with an assertion—"It is my belief that we are just now on the growing edge of an anthropological understanding of law in its various manifestations"—and went on to confess that "the anthropological study of law has not to date affected, in any grand way at least, the theory and methodology of the anthropological discipline" (Nader 1965: 1). Thirty-five years on, the impact of the anthropological study of law on the allied fields of law and social inquiry is undeniable. "Our" terrain—the non-Western cultures we tend to study—our approaches and methods (such as participant observation), and what we have learned about social and cultural processes through ethnography have steadily filtered into other disciplines. Notions of critique and comparison, culture and local knowledge, and various ideas about pluralism and perception also have moved horizontally from anthropology into sister disciplines. Indeed, an interest in one of our key fields of inquiry—the disputing process—has spread beyond the academic world into industry and government in a new manifestation. I use the word "filtered" deliberately because what has been taken from anthropology is often selective, whereas anthropological projects are more encompassing. All the players in disputing are important, but the plaintiff as initiator of complaints holds center stage.

Like most anthropologists in the 1950s, I was trained in the classic mode of science and humanism, in a general anthropology that included society, culture, biology, history, and prehistory as they impinge on the human condition. Sociocultural anthropologists use firsthand methodologies (observations, interviews, documents, etc.) to demonstrate how preliterate oral societies without central authorities maintain social control. When comparison is an issue, anthropologists battle over the use of Western jurisprudential categories such as civil law and criminal law, and these battles in turn move us to describe legal systems in terms of their own epistemological context, especially in the international arena. Repeatedly, the existence of different native categories of law forces us to question the two powerful categories of Western law—"civil" and "criminal"—as cultural constructs that are the legacy of a specific Western lawyering tradition, constructs that today are being transnationalized and biologized by those who think, for example, that there is a criminal gene.

The interaction between anthropology and law is thus not new, as indicated in my second chapter. During the nineteenth century and into the twentieth century, those who seemed most skilled at combining anthropology and law were marginal to their own disciplines and, for this reason perhaps, able to engage in innovative thinking and boundary crossing. And the times were receptive to public intellectuals. In the eighteenth century, European intellectuals had treated law as universal and easily identified in all societies. Nineteenth-century lawyer-anthropologists engaged in armchair work to postulate differences between Western and non-Western law. However, it was not until the twentieth century that actual ethnographic field studies became the norm for sociocultural anthropologists, who thereafter made significant progress in understanding the legal systems of particular societies worldwide. These field studies, pioneered during a period of rapid industrial expansion in the United States and rapid spread of European colonialism worldwide, inspired options for social engineering through law that continue to the present. People could be regulated and administered through law, and law was and is often a means of inventing culture. The debates that ensued often appeared as philosophical issues, though much more is at stake, as we shall see.

In the second half of the nineteenth century, the English jurist Sir Henry Maine engaged in trans-Atlantic skirmishes with the American lawyer and anthropologist Lewis Henry Morgan, debating such matters as theories of history and social evolution and the impact of these theories on democracy versus plutocracy, the position of women, the rights of native peoples, and the justification of the exercise of imperialist powers. By the middle of the twentieth century, the lawyer and the anthropologist represented two separate disciplines. Specialization took hold, inviting a close collaboration between a legal scholar and an anthropologist—Karl Llewellyn, a professor of law, and E. Adamson Hoebel, a professor of anthropology. They were interested not in history but in the contemporary scene and legal reform. Their joint work, *The Cheyenne Way: Conflict and Case*

Law in Primitive Jurisprudence, which appeared in 1941, was one of the first books to examine modern and primitive law in order to subject Western ideas about law to comparative scrutiny for purposes of enhancing the legal realism reform movement. Their book was, in today's parlance, a cultural critique aimed at disturbing the cultural self-satisfaction of rule-bound lawyers. The realists viewed judges and legal scholars as trapped in a formal orientation to rules. Their antilaw rhetoric served as a rationale for law reform, their comparison as seduction.

The academic legal movements that have flourished since the 1970s, namely the Law and Society movement, the Critical Legal Studies movement, the Law in Economics movement, have all involved law and anthropology, with an occasional dash of intellectual activism. What stands abundantly clear in a hundred years of interdisciplinary exchange is the use of different legal paradigms as major engines of change; such paradigms have been used to develop evolutionary theories of rights in property that provide the authority for ownership in connection with imperialism and colonization, to frame the rights of women in a way that enhances Western notions of positional superiority, to argue that law responds to changing conditions (as when experience perforce overrides legal formalism), or to fight to reverse the burden of proof in a highly industrialized world. Yet in spite of clear scholarly argument, theorists of society and culture have not adequately recognized the centrality of law in social change. When the significance of legal hegemonies goes unrecognized, they become even more powerful because they are assumed, quite incorrectly, to be natural or benign. Players in the disputing processes are commonly caught up in these legal hegemonies, which include social *and* cultural controls. When particular emphasis is placed on the cultural modes, the concept of controlling processes is useful in delineating paradigms of legal change, with particular emphasis on who uses the law and for what.

After I entered anthropology in the 1950s, portrayals of indigenous peoples as self-confined and static or as having legal institutions that stood independently from other institutions in their society (such as colonialism) gave way to an emphasis on process models, which connected law to social and cultural structures, to economic and political organization, and to professional habit or religion. The law is not autonomous, we concluded. The process model broadened the angle of vision to include power as a key factor in determining the interactions between different users of law. As a result, disputants were seen as active makers of law, employing their own strategies to steer the legal process. Not surprisingly, power became a central issue in studies of law and studies of the disputing process, and the issues raised by complainants were seen as being about more than just disputing per se.

The broadened meaning of disputing became even clearer as I turned my attention from face-to-face to face-to-faceless societies, where the social distance and power differentials between disputants were so great that entirely new outcomes for parties of unequal power had to be explained. The clash of interests between colonizers, missionaries, and the indigenous people in colonized places caused dynamic tension, as does the clash of interests between consumers and producers of goods and services in modern centralizing contexts. Studies in the political economy of law revealed that the law is not neutral but instead often created by and for the groups in power; a picture of the powerless plaintiff competes with a picture of the powerful plaintiff *as an evolving, not static, phenomenon.*

By the 1980s, ethnographers had developed ethnohistorical models of law that combined history and ethnography within a framework of power structures. Methodologies became increasingly eclectic. One had to consider the phenomenon of world systems, to consider how macrostructures of the 1990s like NAFTA might influence and be influenced by the traditionally studied microstructures or small villages. Could it be that our law, rooted in a small-scale agricultural period in which face-to-face relationships predominated, is no longer appropriate in an industrial society in which so many of the real and potential legal complaints are between strangers of unequal power? Pre-state societies invented a plethora of social and cultural forms of control that we might benefit from knowing about. Today the anthropology of disputing is imbued with a dynamism generated by the notion that culture is more mobile than fixed. Culture as a form of control has become especially relevant to happenings in law. Hegemonies and counterhegemonies, as illustrated in chapter 3, are now critical analytical concepts. A current example of hegemonic power in the United States that I discuss involves the contestation of Native American identity and sovereignty. The invention of Native American culture as harmonious and nonadversarial by insiders and outsiders makes tribal sovereignty an illusion. Absent strict legal guarantees, tribal peoples are susceptible to being manipulated for industrial purposes and, as I show, to becoming willing participants as partners in nuclear waste storage enterprises or as dismissible actors in indigenous challenges over land ownership or intellectual property rights.

Lawyers rarely think about law without also thinking about power, but for Anglo-American anthropologists in particular, macropower was a discovery, and renewed interest in power resulted in studies of global systems and hegemonic theory. Decentered and uneven processes of ideological penetration naturalize the workings of power. Hegemonic ideas can be in flux, constructed and reconstructed by various actors and institutions within diverse social, cultural, and political contexts. Systems of thought reflect the interests of certain classes that attempt to universalize their beliefs and values as they are generated by those involved in the production of culture. Hegemony is an especially useful concept in describing directions of change in law. An interesting revelation in this work on systems of thought was the realization that even the most "scientific" legal observers are limited by the belief systems and thought structures of their own cultures and disciplinary paradigms. Just as in conferences on peacemaking in Africa, participants avoid mentioning arms dealing, multinational corporations, colonial legacies, or mercenary armies, so too in poverty-ridden Oakland, California, professional anger managers omit mention of hunger or inequalities as they rush to put out the fires of conflict in urban schools. The value-ladenness of legal models is apparent—for instance, in the uncritical preference many anthropologists display for harmony legal systems over confrontational or adversarial ones.

The harmony law model plays a complicated role in legal systems and legal theory and is central to much of the story in this book. In chapter 3, I argue that the harmony law model found in Zapotec society may have had its roots in the Spanish colonial period. The model gradually came to be used as a counterhegemonic system that solidified social integration at the local level and helped defend against the encroachment of the Mexican state. In the United States—in large part as a response to the civil rights movements of the 1960s—the harmony law model, or the Alternative Dispute Resolution (ADR) movement (formally launched at the now-famous Pound conference in 1976), seems to function as a pacification plan. It has become part of a major overhaul of the U.S. judicial system in the direction of delegalization. We now discern clearer links between colonialism and the political economy of dispute processing in the modern world. Both use disputing models for purposes of control. As ADR (sometimes referred to as peacemaking or anger management) moves into the international scene of river disputing, as in the case of the Danube, and trade organizations, the settling of international disputes moves from purview of the International Court of Justice at the Hague to that of nongovernmental or supragovernmental groups. The atrophying of law at the international level parallels that at the national level. The movement is from adversarial to negotiation or harmony law models.

In this book, I argue that the life and death of the law derive from the plaintiff, and that this fact is nowhere more important perhaps than in our democratic society. Regardless of whether anthropologists have been able to decide on a strict definition of law that is universal, we have been able to document the universal presence of justice forums. The search for justice is a fundamental part of the human trajectory, although the meaning of justice and its forms varies. Feelings of wrong and right are ubiquitous, as are feelings of injustice. Indeed, social psychologists have argued that the justice motive is a basic human motive that is found in all human societies and is part of many, if not all, human interactions. My concept of a user theory of law suggests that the direction of law is in large measure dependent on who can and wants to use the law, a user process that may expand and contract with the changing political winds. In state systems of law, the plaintiff role atrophies because of the monopoly use of criminal cases by the state. Over time, the role of the civil plaintiff is also endangered by the change in relations associated with industrialized wage-labor and the resultant inequities that stand in the way of equal access to law.

Although the notion that users of law make or create law is not news to lawyers, it has not been on center stage in the social science literature, which as I later note has commonly favored judicial decision-making. This bias has prevented many social scientists from seeing that when plaintiffs act, defendants tend to fight back. When active plaintiffs threaten civil action, there is predictably a power move to close down access; we see this happening today in the United States on the tort issue. It is by means of the plaintiff role that litigation in smaller societies is commonly conceptualized so differently from ours, for in so many places studied by anthropologists, the plaintiff is unencumbered by problems of access or know-how.

The present movement against American tort law is a movement against what is probably the most progressive tort law in the world, one that has been shaped by citizen plaintiffs and plaintiff lawyers who have struggled to force the law to address issues resulting from the industrial and technological innovations of our time. In the eighteenth century, Americans did not need to sue over polluted waters or food or asbestos-related diseases or contaminated agricultural products. In today's technologically centralized society, the burden of proof is central. In a relatively short time, an extraordinary diversity of potentially harmful products has come into daily use—drugs, industrial equipment, intrauterine devices such as the Dalkon Shield—and product liability laws have brought awareness of the need for safer products. Medical malpractice cases have directed attention to the performance of professional services.

As I indicate in my closing chapter, when its users are powerful entities, the law is shaped and becomes hegemonic because their interests are well defined and commonly buttressed by propaganda. The powerful react to challenge. Mass tort cases have increased manufacturers' efforts to reduce the legal protection afforded by trial by jury. On the other hand, lawyers claim that the common law is a dynamic law evolving to meet the changing conditions of society. Yet when users do not speak from positions of dominance, they also do not command the major instruments of private power—that is, the press, marketing companies, and so on. One can, however, speak simultaneously about a "user theory of law" and "hegemony" precisely because powerless users can become a hegemonic force. In 1916, Justice Benjamin Cardozo, in his decision in *MacPherson v. Buick Motor Co.,* signaled the beginnings of a change from a caveat emptor society that places the burden of proof on the unsuspecting consumer to a world that places the burden on the manufacturer:

If the nature of a thing is such that it is reasonably certain to place life and limb in peril when negligently made, it is then a thing of danger. Its nature gives warning of the consequences to be expected. If to the element of danger then is added knowledge that the thing will be used by persons other than the purchasers and used without new tests, then, irrespective of contract, the manufacturer of this thing of danger is under a duty to make it carefully. (1916: 389–90)

This decision provoked plaintiff activities in the twentieth century and will continue to stimulate action in the twenty-first. Without the civil plaintiff, citizens are only defendants. When the state reigns supreme, we enter into lawlessness, and the legitimacy of law is challenged in societies that place great emphasis on individual rights and basic freedoms, such as the right of individuals to regulate their own affairs, as in the law of contracts. Litigation can keep a democratic society healthy. Class action, or multidistrict litigation, is what makes litigation possible in a mass society, and implemented legislation may prevent disputing in the first place.

The human condition can be more fully understood only when we recognize the justice motive as a powerful drive in defining the directions of law and of society itself. More specifically, we need to think about the implications of a rhetoric of consensus, homogeneity, and agreement and about the contradictions such a rhetoric poses for a society that espouses the ideal of the rule of law as a cornerstone of democratic order, a society whose worldwide expansion and influence touch the lives of so many previously excluded groups.

ONE

Evolving an Ethnography of Law
A Personal Document

> An ethnographer who sets out to study only religion, or only
> technology, or only social organization cuts out an artificial field
> for inquiry, and he will be seriously handicapped in this work.
>
> *Bronislaw Malinowski*

I began my first fieldwork in 1957, during a quieter, slower
period, a time when an anthropologist had some degree of iso-
lation—or so it appeared. I was supported by a Mexican government grant of approximately $1,200 to cover all expenses for
nine months' fieldwork in Oaxaca, Mexico. My project was to
study a region as yet unexplored by either anthropologists or
historians, and to focus on the question of settlement densities
in order to find out how settlement patterns affect forms of
social organization. The project was a fairly general one, but
then my training had been general rather than specialized.
When I arrived in Oaxaca, I learned of the work of the Pa-

paloapan Commission, a Mexican development agency, and of the work of that commission in the Rincón Zapotec area, where I was headed. The engineer in charge of road building took me into Rincón Zapotec territory, at least as far as the road went, and left me there at the end of the road with the locals.

As I walked along a mountain trail behind two monolingual Zapotec guides, I wondered what on earth had brought me to this remote place. I was dimly aware of the settlements enfolded by the mountains in view. Orchids bloomed in abundance that May before the rainy season began. Suddenly we were in Talea, a large village of vivid green contrasted with the adobe houses, surrounded by coffee plants in flower. My guides led me to houses of friends of the engineer, a family that had tentatively agreed to take me in. Those first few days were paradise. Not only was I finally in the field, but the place was breathtakingly beautiful.

But then the village's Catholic priest accused me from the pulpit of being a Protestant missionary. The engineer from the Papaloapan voyaged from Oaxaca to vouch for me, but his corroboration of my story helped only a little. The rosy beginning had been spoiled, and the suspicions were to be followed by other accusations. Tension grew worse when I became sick with malaria and hepatitis. Fieldwork is a series of trials and errors and tribulations; one cycles from anguish to exultation.[1]

Today when my students go to the jungles of Peru, Bolivia, Guatemala, Indonesia, Mexico, they trip all too frequently over

1. In 1970, a brief description of my first two field experiences, "From Anguish to Exultation," was published in a collection of such reports titled *Women in the Field* and edited by Peggy Golde.

NGOs (nongovernmental organizations), corporate enterprises, missionaries, military personnel, tourists and treasure seekers, and native peoples who want something in return for serving as research material. As times change, as questions and methodologies change, it becomes doubly important for the anthropologist to be eclectic, flexible, and free of any rigid canon.

In these changing times, when trends are so powerful and when anthropologists have allied themselves with other disciplines working on law and society, something has disappeared from the essence of anthropology and ethnography. While questioning the assumptions of the researcher and using analytical frames of a wide-angle variety, we seem to ignore crafting experience. Everyone must, it seems, start anew. Perhaps some useful ideas that several generations of anthropologists have taken for granted should be reaffirmed more clearly. Bronislaw Malinowski put it to us many years ago: "An ethnographer who sets out to study only religion, or only technology, or only social organization cuts out an artificial field for inquiry, and he will be seriously handicapped in his work" (1926:11). Malinowski's admonition is especially relevant to the ethnographic study of law (or the study of law as an anthropological document) today, when it is fashionable to equate ethnography with qualitative work or with "hanging out," or to understand law only in relation to its most immediate and specialized context. My training as an anthropologist led me to approach the study of law in a manner altogether distinct from that of a psychologist, sociologist, or researcher with principally legal training. In my first exposure to Rincón Zapotec society, I faced a baffling set of unknowns that left me without a frame of reference. Nevertheless, by heeding Malinowski's admonition and the observations of other ethnographers, I was able to remove my own notions of law in my first work among the Zapotec and somewhat later among the Shia Muslims of south Lebanon. When thrust into another society, one can either fall back on one's own culture and transpose it onto the other and get into a real mess, or one can be an ethnographer. At that moment, underpinning everything was ethnography.

When I entered anthropology, I found that conflict had had and continued to have an ambivalent place in sociocultural anthropology. Turn-of-the-century British anthropologists working in Australia had thought they must return to camp if there was fighting among the Aborigines instead of staying to observe, but by midcentury in British anthropology, the Manchester school, led by Max Gluckman, was arguing that social conflict was functional for the maintenance of social systems. At the same time, in the United States, anthropologists Bernard Siegal and Alan Beals represented conflict as a dysfunctional process produced by strains and stresses in the social system. In the early 1960s, the sources of conflict, as well as its functional value, were conceptualized in terms of broad understandings of social organization, religion, economic interdependence, and political structures. By 1968, Ralf Dahrendorf had extended the argument to point out that societies are held together not by consensus but by constraint, not by universal agreement but by the coercion of some by others. Nevertheless, by the 1970s, the dialogue over conflict and harmony was shifting once again. Conflict was now portrayed as uncivilized. The study of law was then marginal in anthropology. Yet even as I attempted to breathe new life into the field of anthropology of law, I predicted that the field would die if our work was successful, exactly because—as Malinowski has advised—artificial fields of inquiry seriously handicap the ethnographer. Pushing the boundaries is what anthropologists do if they are not trapped in topical or other specialities, or in hegemonic paradigms.

FIELDWORK SITES

My fieldwork sites have been diverse, but among the Rincón Zapotec peoples, I learned to study disputing in law courts in the context of the wider social and cultural organization of two small villages. I did so almost by accident, because my first research topic centered on spatial organization and social control. I found the best indicators of differences in my comparative study of two Zapotec mountain villages, one dispersed, the other compact, in court materials (Nader 1964b). It was among these Zapotec-speaking peoples that I met the plaintiffs who introduced me firsthand to the justice motive. It was here also that I had the immersion so often connected with traditional fieldwork and with doing what it takes to write an ethnography—I spent eighteen months or more there between 1957 and 1969 and have made intermittent visits since 1969. Although long-term ethnographic work does not guarantee success, it allows the possibility of getting at process (rather than just patterns) and allows the ethnographer to identify with, as well as observe, those they study and among whom they live.

In 1957 among the Rincón Zapotec, I was working with several assumptions about order and disorder and working more or less within what some call a positivist model: this model holds that disputes for any particular society are limited in range (that is, not all societies fight about all the possible things human beings could fight about); that a limited number of formal procedures are used by human societies in the prevention or settlement (or avoidance) of grievances (e.g., courts, contests, ordeals, go-betweens); and finally that there will be a choice among a number of modes of settlement (negotiation, mediation, arbitration, adjudication, "lumping it," and so on). Resolving or managing conflicting interests and remedying strife situations are problems that all societies have to deal with, and usually peoples find not one but many ways to handle grievances. What are those ways and do they interrelate?

A number of empirical questions also guided my early work. What did people fight and argue about publicly? Who initiated disputes, and what was the outcome for the individual as well as for the society? Within what groups were disputes concentrated? How did disputes at one level of organization affect those at another? And what were the manifest and hidden jobs of the law, and how were they related to the social structure? I envisioned a qualitative and quantitative sampling of dispute cases. The law case was my focus because I knew that the case in some form (dramatic or mundane) is present in every society: there are always parties who articulate complaints against others (though whether I would discover any particular procedure such as adjudication was uncertain). Furthermore, I thought that mapping the component parts of a case would produce results that could prove useful as a springboard for comparative work. This was the heyday of componential analysis, and I was attracted by the idea of transposing the linguistic notion of a scant number of units to the law case. Little did I realize that the passion of the litigants could not be converted into minimal units.

In the 1950s, the case method was the dominant method in legal anthropology and, for that matter, in other areas within anthropology, both as a means of collecting data and as a tool for analysis. The case method in legal contexts was popularized by Llewellyn and Hoebel (1941). Their use of the case (a focus on a particular action in law) to elicit how the law regulates, prevents, and cleans up "social messes" appealed to me, even as I realized its inadequacies. Later J. F. Holleman (1986) illustrated the limitations of such a method by referring to trouble-less cases—matters that are not disputes, such as patterns of land use and allocation that result in hierarchical relations. Holleman contends that dispute cases are unduly restricted and are bound to lead to an "uneven coverage of the total field of law" (118), a fact that I was deeply aware of in the early 1960s. In recent decades, as von Benda-Beckmann (1986) is quite correct in observing, anthropologists have tended to focus on the coercive side of law, perhaps as a reaction to the preceding era of equilibrium models.

My concern with the case method converged on the boundedness of the case, as it was being used by Hoebel and Gluckman, rather than on its ripple effect. Focusing on the trouble-case does not necessarily prevent the researcher from examining the case in the context of the wider social and cultural processes. Indeed, the use of an extended case method led back into the broader realm of control and order. This expanded meaning of "trouble" indicated that the ethnography of law was "a theory-building part of social anthropology" (Starr and Collier 1989, 6), that dealt with more than "law."

I was influenced by Elizabeth Colson's work on the dispute cases of the Plateau Tonga of Zambia (1953), in which she in-

dicated how crosscutting loyalties contribute to order, something A. L. Kroeber had recorded in his early study of the Zuni
Indians (1917). In many societies, conflicting ties of loyalty, in
addition to ties based on reciprocal exchange, function to pres-
sure disputing parties to end their quarrels. Colson described
the way these processes of control relate to structural or kinship
considerations, and to the importance of a litigant's strategies
for manipulating the structure. Her work centered not so much
on law as on other processes of social control, not so much on
decision-making actors as on the entire system of control in
which actors operated in roles of primary, secondary, or tertiary
importance. That the Tongans were acephalous politically—
that is, they had no centralized political organizations—had
less bearing on the manner in which they handled conflict in
this instance than did the cross-linking features of their social
organization.

The idea of generating comparisons meant that I would have
to develop concepts and ideas that were more or less transcul-
tural; Western jurisprudential ideas would not do as categories
for use in comparing "non-Western" cultures. In the 1950s, the
stage was already set for the debates on ethnographic representation and translation by the exchange between Max Gluckman
and Paul Bohannan. Gluckman (1955) analyzed the Lozi's legal
rationality through their legal decisions, but he underlined the
similarities of Barotse and Western legal institutions by using
Western legal terminology (e.g., right-duty, reasonable man,
corpus juris, etc.). He wanted to show that the Barotse were
not "savages," that their legal concepts were sophisticated. He
also tried to grasp the changes this system was undergoing by
looking at the flexibility and the "certainty of the uncertainty"

in the verdicts of judges, and he used the importance of time and exchange to explain legal change. Bohannan's *Justice and Judgement among the Tiv* (1957) starts by describing the structure of courts in Nigeria. Though Bohannan explains the colonial origin of the system of courts in Nigeria, he presents the co-existing indigenous and nonindigenous courts as separate systems. In this scheme, his insistence on calling the Tiv's a folk legal system makes sense. Lack of codification or systematization of "law" and "custom" among the Tiv made it impossible for him to compare the Western folk term "law" with any Tiv term or concept. Bohannan emphatically points out that "Tiv have 'laws,' but do not have 'law'" (57). They settle disputes not according to rules, which do not exist, but according to their cultural understanding. The aim of Tiv laws was to obtain rights.

Behind Bohannan's and Gluckman's inquiries is a concern for the authenticity of our ethnographies. How much do we as anthropologists alter our subject matter when we attempt to describe, analyze, or compare? In the end, whether we apply Western legal concepts depends on whether we understand law as autonomous or embedded. If, on the one hand, law were independent from society, then law could be universal. Western categories are independent of their original context. On the other hand, if law were dependent, then applying Western legal concepts would distort ethnographic data. From this point of view, the case method was a problem. In other words, I thought long and hard about what it would take to carry out an ethnography of law and what the pitfalls might be. And there were certainly pitfalls.

Among the Mexican Rincón Zapotec, my study of social relations and social groups took me into the town courts, and the town court cases took me outside the court into the community and into other communities, especially if the disputes were between inhabitants of different villages. This kind of expansion is what is meant by the extended case method. In addition, however, I closely observed daily activities bearing on subsistence, life cycle, politics, music, health and sickness, kinship, fiestas, and projects of development. Again, I was aware that in ethnography, focal concerns must be broadly contextualized. In my focus on disputing, I used the extended case approach that had been found useful in African work, carried out interviews, engaged in participant observation, gathered census data, and used archival documents—anything (quantitative or qualitative) that I could get my hands on—in order to produce what we then thought of as a holistic ethnography. I took seriously the admonition that setting out to study only law (in whatever form it might take) cuts out an artificial field for inquiry that handicaps scholarly research. An ethnographic study of law is more than a study of judicial institutions, and legal systems themselves constitute only parts of larger systems (Nader and Yngvesson 1974). Ethnography is the science of context.

I reiterate that, as viewed from anthropology, the law cannot usefully be isolated from other social and cultural systems of control that serve many purposes—from settling conflicts to pacification to creating conformity with norms, or to outright warfare. The values that are tested, changed, and consolidated in the law are not necessarily or even exclusively "legal values" They may be religious, aesthetic, or economic values. The law may function to maintain an unequal distribution of power or material wealth, or it may be used to bring about a more nearly equitable distribution of resources. Litigation may be a means of social control, or it may be a game that links social units in a common social activity. In other words, an anthropological study of law knows no boundaries, and therefore it challenges preconceived notions about the autonomous nature of law, notions that it is "unaffected by social and economic relations, political forces, and cultural phenomena," notions that mask the existence of ideological myths (Kairys 1982: 6).

Fieldwork, then, is more than participant observation, and producing an ethnography of law entails a good deal more than collecting cases. Of course, any ethnography will be only partial, but I aimed for the most holistic (though partial) ethnography of law that I could produce (Nader 1990). I made more than a dozen trips back to the Rincón while thinking and writing about these issues. My film *To Make the Balance* (Nader 1966) moved my attention from social relations to styles of court procedure (Nader 1969a), and in 1981 the Public Broadcasting Associates and I made a second film, titled *Little Injustices,* in which we tried to contrast Zapotec complaint handling with that of an industrialized country, the United States. I came to understand the Zapotec situation better partly because over the years I became involved in other studies of law in the United States and elsewhere.

After all was said and done, what resulted from my work with the Zapotec was more than a localized ethnography (Nader 1990). It was a thick description that theorized what I term the "harmony law model," a configuration of compromise, reconciliation, and win-win solutions. It was a study in the political economy of legal cultures. To understand the hegemony, I had put to one side the possibility of yet more ethnographic research and set about the task of examining historical and comparative documents that dealt with Christian missionizing and European colonialism, subjects that I and others had ignored in earlier decades. Only then could I develop a more comprehensive theory of village law. What I discovered was the use of the harmony law model as a means of pacification through law, first as a requirement of conquest, then as a counterhegemonic response by the indigenes to more than five hundred years of dealing with colonization.

My first Zapotec study taught me the basics of ethnography: not all fieldwork is ethnographic (as when one depends solely on survey research, for example), and "fieldwork" and "ethnography" are terms that should not be used interchangeably. Nor should ethnography value qualitative over quantitative methods. Both are needed. I also understood better why anthropologists are averse to spelling out their fieldwork methods with greater prior specificity. We needed to prepare for the unexpected, and we needed to be flexible in order to do so. Our stance was not to be static or rigid. We were taught that searching for the "native's point of view," that is, differentiating between what people say they do and what the ethnographer observes they do, and doing so in depth and with a wide angle, require a set of techniques and methods for gathering and analyzing data that includes not only "background issues" but also both quantitative and qualitative divides. An ethnographer could be both positivist and interpretivist, a sociocultural scientist and a humanist simultaneously. Relevant to the period was the reissue of Gregory Bateson's *Naven* (1958). Bateson's arguments against false paradigm oppositions suited my eclectic temperament.

I started by trying to figure out how the mountain Zapotec courts worked in southern Mexico. I needed to know something about the organizational context in which they were set. After my early work on the social organization of two Zapotec villages and the systems of social control of which the courts were a part (Nader 1964b), I became interested in participation patterns in the courts, and the data collection became even more systematic: I collected court records and an analysis of these records to answer the how many, who, and what questions. My most striking findings lay in the broad array of participation and particularly in how women used the courts (Nader 1985). In the process of this counting work, I noticed that a high litigation rate was accompanied by a harmony ideology, a pattern of dispute settlement dominated by compromise and conciliation. Why? There were internalist explanations of a structural-functional sort: the people were so divided that they needed a culture of harmony to hold them together, or some such explanations related to cultural control. I could see no justification for setting the problem up as a hypothesis for testing. Harmony was a cultural theme that penetrated the talk of village life but not the behavior observed in courtroom encounters. It struck me that I could not adequately address this question either by thinking harder about the Zapotec data I had collected or by collecting more data; the answer was not to be found in an internalist analysis, whether structural-functionalist or mentalist. It struck me that different ways of knowing do come in waves in anthropology, although they might be used simultaneously. Eric Wolf, in *Europe and the People without History* (1982), had noticed: "The more ethnohistory we know, the more clearly 'their' history and 'our' history emerge as part of the same history" (19). I realized that the interest in small-scale and seemingly autonomous communities gives way to comparisons between seemingly autonomous communities and, later, to an interest in the diffusion of ideas pertaining to law, diffusion that has Europeans emerge as part of the same history as that of the contemporary Zapotec. Though I had been able to describe law and the uses of harmony law models among the Talean Zapotec, my analysis gathered power only when I placed the particular in a global context, one in which Christianity and colonialism and the resistances and adaptations to these global movements were incorporated and brought to bear on our understanding of the small scale.

It was the search for higher levels of understanding that inspired me to move from local to global. My methods took on more in the style of a natural science approach: *the questions were driving the methods.* To understand the meaning of harmony within a persistently litigious population, I had to search the historical literature for data on colonial and contemporary interactions between missionizing Christians and styles of disputing. To comprehend the worldwide diffusion of an ideology of harmony required comparative consciousness and awareness of the diffusion of idea systems, as well as a realization that the mountain Zapotec village that I was studying reflected hundreds of years of colonial experience continuing into the contemporary period. I moved from studying mechanisms of *social* control with an emphasis on social relationships to studying mechanisms of *cultural* control with greater attention to the ideational, mechanisms that may have emanated from locales a great distance from the isolated mountain village. This new realization made me rethink the critiques of structural-functionalist approaches. The "enduring structures" described by anthropologists were part of the natives' presentation of self to outsiders, part of their adaptation to systems of domination. Viewed in this light, indigenous legal systems appear to be in equilibrium, or balanced, or harmonious. The realization that the social and cultural fields were broader than the small community compelled me to include dynamic forces that played upon and affected community contours that, though not constructed by the mountain Zapotec, were now being used by them.

Of course, harmony can come in many forms: it may be part of a local tradition of intimacy and interconnectedness or part of systems of control that have diffused across the world along with colonialism, Christianity, and other macroscale systems of cultural control such as psychotherapy. The basic components of harmony as ideology are the same wherever it appears as cultural control: the emphasis on avoidance and conciliation, the belief that conflict resolution is inherently good and that its opposite, continued conflict or controversy, is bad or dysfunctional, the belief that peaceful, orderly behavior is more civilized than confrontative behavior, the belief that consensus is of greater survival value than controversy. Such beliefs are deeply embedded in Western social science literature, and every few decades we get a plea to notice that it is "not the presence but the absence of conflict that is surprising and abnormal" (Dahrendorf 1968: 127).

The story of ideology formation is at the start nebulous. In the case of harmony among the Talean Zapotec, I speculate in my book *Harmony Ideology* (1990) about how ideologies of control evolved from a colonial Spanish America, and I extrapolate from the comparative evidence on colonialism and customary law more generally. There is little doubt that the missionary activities in Oaxaca past and present and the zeal of the missionary orders affected the basic ideological structures of the native populations. The Spanish conquest was in good part a spiritual conquest (Ricard 1966), and the "missions of penetration" spread into areas where Spanish political control had not yet been installed.

An examination of village social life and the workings of village law courts among the mountain Zapotec reveals the heritage of penetration. The processes of internal and external forces appear in the interconnectedness of social organization and in the actual disputing process in and out of the Zapotec court system. We come to understand the broader meaning of the use of harmony and equilibrium as political strategies and as ideologies. We also come to understand how such processes of equilibrium and conflict can influence the theories of the people who study them—the anthropologists. My conclusion that among the Talean Zapotec a hegemonic harmony tradition stems from Spanish and Christian influence (a tradition apart from organic harmony) led me to propose that the uses of harmony are political. But could I verify this conclusion? By what means could I confirm my interpretations?

Anthropological theory is shaped not only by the Western world but also by the ideologies presented by informants. That such ideologies may have had Western origins in the first place becomes even more interesting as we attempt to trace the sources of anthropological ideas and to answer the question of why Taleans employ the principles of harmony and balance in dispute settlement and in dealings with outsiders. Although initially I focused on how the "natives" use harmony, the issue has brought me to an exploration of harmony ideology as a tool of cultural control in colonial and neocolonial contexts. Changes from harmony law models to confrontational or adversarial law models and back have been documented by historians for a number of societies. In sixteenth-century Castile, compromise, the ideal and preferred means of ending disputes, shifted to the adversary process with changes set into motion by economic expansion and population growth (Kagan 1981). In New Guinea, the opposite may have been happened (Gordon and Meggitt 1985), and in the United States there have been oscillations between harmony and adversarial styles in law (Auerbach 1983). Differing cultural constellations, both indigenous and European, indicate the double impact of Christian missions and colonial courts on the consequent ubiquity of harmony law models. Harmony law models are coercive when they mandate unity, consensus, cooperation, compliance, passivity, and docility—features often taken for granted as humankind's normal state and considered benign. And when Martin Chanock (1985) uses the term "missionary justice" to call attention to the fact that, from the early 1800s, missionaries in Africa were heavily involved in the settlement of disputes, combining biblical law with English procedures as they knew them, he is implying that compromise in colonial African "customary law" became the politics of adjustment and the politics of survival.

Materials from the Pacific region indicate that harmony law was similarly shaped and institutionalized there. Before colonial pacification, a tolerance for or even an enjoyment of quarreling was observed in New Guinea. More recent research documents how evangelical rhetoric affected disputing processes, undercutting traditional means of social harmony and replacing them with Christian harmony. In contemporary Papua New Guinea, ethnographers describe the stratigraphy of legal influences within the added state dimension (Gordon and Meggitt 1985) and in response to economic development. It is in the Fourth World that we can see today the daily shaping power of religion and economics on law.

In an elegant description of present-day examples in Indonesia and Papua New Guinea (PNG), David Hyndman (1994) illustrates how a state faced with a debt crisis favors investors who plunder natural resources and cast indigenous peoples in the role of subversive criminals, peoples seen by anthropologists as having taken up arms to protect their cultural and ancestral homelands. The Indonesian state and PNG, in collusion with transnationals, entered New Guinea to mine gold and copper in a process that Hyndman calls economic development by invasion. The cost of resisting invasion is heavy. In New Guinea, local peoples fought the foreign presence, blockading airstrips and blowing up pipes running from the mines. Lives were lost, property destroyed. Forced resettlement often followed, and local people became trespassers in their own land. Hyndman's story documents one invasion after another, and he notes ironically that Third World colonialism has replaced First World colonialism. Those who resist are considered criminals and are prosecuted under state laws favoring investors.

But law evolves, and contradictory legal values do not always remain in collision. Observations of mountain Zapotec court activity in Mexico indicate that some Zapotec operate with a harmony law model that is similar to legal systems often found where colonialism and Christianity have moved together.

Among these people, enduring relations, culture structures, and world systems interact in ways that result in legal styles of conciliation that have structural equilibrium as their goal. But what may have entered as part of a hegemonic system of European control has evolved in Zapotec country into a counterhegemonic system that serves to solidify social integration at the local level and to erect a legal defense system against encroachment of superordinate control in the form of the state. This picture is now undergoing dramatic change as Mexican resources become internationalized under international trade agreements such as NAFTA and GATT, and our interests, and perhaps our scholarship, will mirror these changes, as will those of the mountain Zapotec.

My second fieldsite was located in Lebanon. Indeed, I always seemed to be working in more than one fieldsite at a time. I went to Lebanon in the aftermath of the landing of the U.S. Marines in 1958. During the summer of 1961, supported by a small grant from the University of California, I located a Shia Muslim village in south Lebanon near both the Syrian and the Israeli borders, a village in which I collected oral cases of conflict using Arabic, in which I was relatively fluent, as the primary language. It was a preliminary to a more general inquiry into the contemporary state of Islamic law in rural settings, an inquiry that unfortunately was aborted by the Israeli military occupation of southern Lebanon a few years later.

My argument was straightforward. Given that Islamic law was originally of chiefly urban origin, I wondered whether customary law predominated over Islamic law in rural settings. In spite of the short duration of my fieldwork, in two and a half months I was able to answer my original question: an ethnographer can be more efficient the second time around because of prior experience with observational techniques and interviews, and self-confidence. I was also able in a short time to generate a model of rural-urban networking around customary law, which unlike Islamic law, operated across the religious lines of Islam and Christianity (Nader 1965b). Although the future of customary law is even today not clear in the Middle East, or in Africa or elsewhere (indeed the very definition of customary law is in question), this short field experience, more than my secluded stay with the Zapotec, sensitized me to the different layers of law that are present wherever anthropologists go. Far from being neat and parallel, these layers of the law merge and diverge, reflecting an intermingling of legal practices (as in south Lebanon) that is continuous and ongoing everywhere in the world, including the United States. Nevertheless, together these two field experiences provided data for comparison of two relatively homogeneous communities of similar size and population, both with cash crop economies, coffee and tobacco, both homogenous in religion—Catholic Zapotec and Shia Muslim; together they allowed me to understand better the connection between social organization and institutions for conflict management. It was a neat "controlled" comparison: one village was characterized by dual organization and the absence of third parties, the other by cross-linkages and a court system.

In Lebanon I also watched how informal systems operated. Busloads of villagers would arrive at a political intermediary's house early in the morning and be ushered into the bedroom, where husband and wife were still in bed having their first cup of coffee. Wives were sympathetic listeners to these highly motivated potential plaintiffs. It was a well-thought-out and accepted strategy to enter the most personal place in the house of a potential intermediary to plead one's case (during which the wife could also intervene on behalf of the complainant). Nothing so personal occurred among the Zapotec, although informal contacts were often made prior to court appearances.

THE BERKELEY VILLAGE LAW PROJECT

The experience of working in Lebanon reinforced the importance of comparison, but I also realized that because each worker was working independently, much of the ethnographic material on law could not be used easily. There was a need for some kind of common framework of inquiry. The idea of using comparison as a method for discovery in the 1960s inspired the Berkeley Village Law Project (Nader 1995; Nader and Todd 1978). Already in the 1960s and 1970s, widespread controversy over the fairness of the American justice system and similar controversy over the fate of indigenous legal systems in the newer nations adopting Western notions of development made the cross-cultural study of law processes a significant and timely subject. The ethnography-of-law approach that I had developed from study and practice was applied and expanded by students working in very different communities. This work reflected an inclination of anthropological interest toward including the cultural as well as the social foundations of order, as well as interest in the reactive processes of law (von Benda-Beckman 1986: 92). The resulting book, *The Disputing Process* (Nader and Todd 1978), is about what people in different cultures do with their "legal" problems in the context of nation-state law. The work was not limited to the study of official legal procedure available to litigants; it was delimited by the avenues actually chosen or developed by the litigants themselves.

Over a twenty-year period, graduate students from Berkeley went to fourteen different locales to study the disputing *process*.[2] My students examined disputing processes using standards of fieldwork of long duration, still concentrating on the collection and analysis of dispute cases within the context of social and cultural organization in small, relatively bounded communities. I visited four of these field-workers in the fieldsites in Lebanon, Liechtenstein, and Mexico. Our most important findings centered on conditions under which different forms or styles of dispute management occur. For example, mediation between parties of greatly unequal power does not work. Again, context provided clues as to why styles of conflict decision-making varied within each culture, as well as between cultures. In the process, it also became clear that rapidly developing countries were changing anthropological views that the local level was in any way isolated from the impact of larger political and eco-

2. Several of these anthropologists published monograph-length books on this work: Klaus-Friedrich Koch, *War and Peace in Jalémó: The Management of Conflict in Highland New Guinea* (1974); Phillip C. Parnell, *Escalating Disputes: Social Participation and Change in the Oaxacan Highlands* (1988); June Starr, *Dispute and Settlement in Rural Turkey: An Ethnography of Law* (1978), and *Law as Metaphor: From Islamic Courts to the Palace of Justice* (1992); Nancy Williams, *Two Laws: Managing Disputes in a Contemporary Aboriginal Community* (1987), and *The Yolngu and Their Land: A System of Land Tenure and the Fight for Its Recognition* (1986); and Cathy Witty, *Mediation and Society: Conflict Management in Lebanon* (1980).

nomic structures. Believing that prior approaches to dispute management put too much emphasis on equilibrium and shared interests, the anthropologists in the Berkeley Village Law Project studied disputing processes as part of networks of shifting social relations and cultural paradigms. Unlike other anthropological studies of law, the work followed a common model in data collection, focusing on dimensions of disputing as they affected the litigant's choice of remedy agent: the network of social relations, the control of scarce resources, the distribution of power, the aims of the participating actors, access to forums, timing, cost, the cultural dimension, and the degree of incorporation into national legal systems.

The ten ethnographers who wrote chapters for *The Disputing Process* present a wide diversity, from groups that have virtually no contact with nation-state law to societies that exemplify the increasing incorporation of state law into local traditional systems, from societies with little or no use of third parties to societies that make regular use of courts or other third-party mechanisms. Between 1965 and 1975, members of the Berkeley Village Law Project encompassed ethnography of law in fourteen locales—Jalé of Indonesian New Guinea; a Scandinavian fishing village; urban Ghana; a Sunni Muslim village; a multireligious village in Lebanon; and peasant villages in Bavaria, Turkey, Sardinia, Zambia, and Mexico, as well as locales in the United States, Ecuador, Liechtenstein, and Australia that were not reported on in the volume. Each study analyzes the ways in which disputes are settled primarily from the point of view of the litigant(s). And while much of the behavior is familiar and linked to the concerns of people in modern nation states, the authors set out to explain why the disputing process looks different to each of the participants, how different procedures are limited, what factors affect access, and the manner in which nation-state law intersects with local-level law. The Berkeley project was an achievement in systematic intrasocietal comparison. By probing agency and power relationships within these various societies, the work provides pointed contrasts on how law functions in more-complex arenas, but it was not the end of the story. Laurel Rose (1992), the last anthropologist of the Berkeley project, broke new ground with her work on ideology and land dispute strategies.

MOVING ON: THE BERKELEY COMPLAINT PROJECT

The fieldwork that paralleled the Berkeley Village Law Project was a break from the usual small and localized anthropological fieldsite. For the first time, I began to work in the country of which I was a citizen and to ask how people in a mass society like the United States complain about products and services and with what consequences. *The Disputing Process* was about disputes between people of the same culture, who for the most part knew each other and were expected to interact in some fashion in the future regardless of the outcome of the dispute. I then turned to disputes between people who were strangers to each other. This study, based on work in the United States between 1970 and 1980, again involved numerous researchers who looked at what Americans did when they had or perceived that they had no access to law. Central to the organization of this project was the complaint letter. Americans are probably the most prolific complaint-letter writers in the world.

I began this work in the early to mid-1970s, somewhat by chance; I was given the opportunity to examine a large corpus of letters written by people who felt they had been shafted by the system, and I realized that these letters threw a powerful searchlight onto what was happening as Americans faced the evolution of a system of justice in a world in which face-to-face relationships were almost non-existent. Some of my colleagues argued that there was no way anyone could turn such material into the basis for ethnographic inquiry; the challenge for me was to find one. Students were attracted to this project and came from universities and colleges around the country (Harvard and Williams, among others), as well as from Berkeley: students who had fresh minds and were prepared to tackle big issues, students who were still imbued with a belief that they could make a difference in the world. This project required me to pay attention for the first time to the law literature of this country: as always, when an anthropologist enters new territory, he or she must master a new body of literature.

From the letters, my students and I learned that people who felt unfairly treated and yet had no access to legal protection sought redress through a variety of "third-party intermediaries," from neighborhood consumer complaint offices to media action lines, to department store complaint desks, to unions, to consumer action groups, to their congressional representatives, to the White House Office of Consumer Affairs. The persistence and inventiveness in their pursuit of justice, even after they had seemingly exhausted all avenues, was extraordinary. Thereupon, we began the ethnographic profiling of the numbers of these complaint cases, as well as the organizations to which they were taken for hearing. The extended case histories of these complaints indicated a legacy of frustration, of mistrust, of apprehension. The implications of the uneven struggle that took place daily in a million ways between individuals and institutions, I observed, were adding up to no less than what someone called the "slow death of justice" in the United States. Those complaining were, after all, believers in "the system," and as one complainant said in the *Little Injustices* film, "There's gotta be some justice somewhere."

Who were these complainants? How did they plan their strategies? How did they learn where to take a problem pertaining to law? Most of our research was invested in these life histories of consumer complaints about corporate products and services and what people thought was a big or little injustice, and what alternatives existed in government, unions, organizations, the media, and grassroots efforts. Our investigations revealed a mass phenomenon in which large segments of the population, reflecting all socioeconomic groups, are exposed to low-profile, undramatic, petty exploitations that may have serious consequences: a defective stove that burns down a home or a lemon car that leaves the family breadwinner paralyzed. When there is no access to law, extrajudicial processes develop directly in response to the decline in activity of the civil plaintiff. The U.S. courts have so far refused to extend to civil litigants the constitutional right to counsel that is guaranteed to criminal defendants.

Our conclusions were not relevant solely to United States citizens. Struggles in our highly evolved industrial country over the problems of how to achieve consumer satisfaction in terms of health and safety as well as dollars invested were emerging in similar ways worldwide with the global spread of consumerism. If one follows the birth of fledgling consumer complaint mechanisms worldwide, one does begin to believe that there is indeed a justice motive (Lerner 1975) operating universally.

Both Berkeley projects cast law in the context of operating processes of social and cultural control, and our understanding of these controls was again to be cast in the broader dynamic of the culture and social spheres of the locales in question. The complaint study focused on the interaction of different law actors or users of law and the networks they spawned. We developed a processual model by which we pursued the social dimensions of a case beyond the borders of the manifest dispute to classes of complaints normally hidden from view until they appear as class actions, as with the asbestos and the Dalkon Shield cases. The approaches included an analysis of power relations, and the interaction between the users and their power relative to one another became key factors in understanding how users change, or fail to change, the asymmetry. The focus on remedy agents to whom one carried a complaint was limited and allowed for numbers of field-workers using traditional anthropological methods to examine a number of remedy agents who worked in response to the complainant. Much had been written about the problem of no access or delayed access to U.S. courts, and various remedies had been offered, some leading to the development of small claims courts, regulatory agencies, and public interest law firms. But with the exception of Gellhorn (1966) and a small number of other researchers, few had asked exactly how people with no access to law handled their complaints. What we began to uncover was only the tip of the iceberg. Much had been written about alienation but not much about the actual means by which people became alienated.

Much had been written about the silent majority, but no one knew whether Americans were silent or whether they were silenced, for we had no adequate knowledge about where Americans spoke and were heard.

One theme running through the book that resulted from this work, *No Access to Law: Alternatives to the American Judicial System* (Nader 1980), was that of consumers deeply disillusioned with government and corporations. Typically, consumers who did complain had begun their search for remedy as firm believers in "the system"; they believed it would give them redress. After enduring rebuffs and getting the runaround, they lost faith, often retreating into anger, or apathy; but sometimes they went all the way, learned about the system, and won. Although our research was geared to discover instances in which third-party handlers were successful, we concluded that our society had not evolved effective systems for dealing with grievances that may be small but have critical consequences. In other words, law had not adapted to the transformation of a rural society into a mass industrial society. In conclusion, the researchers rank-ordered the effectiveness of intermediaries in handling grievances. Among the third-party intermediaries we examined—including a local better business bureau , a state insurance department, an automobile manufacturer, a labor union, a congressional office—the most effective were those rare organizations, such as department stores, that provided complainants with face-to-face opportunities to resolve their disputes.

This several-year study of mass consumer phenomena yielded both observations and recommendations. All the ethnographers were citizens of the country they were studying (that is, they had rights to know), and the funding agency encouraged a search for successful solutions to marketplace complaints. The study itself was an early multisited research project that used ethnographic work to survey how Americans complained and with what consequence (Nader, *No Access,* 1980), a subject that forced me into the law library. The book was followed by the PBS documentary on my work, *Little Injustices* (1981). This film, in the Odyssey series, contrasted easy access to remedy in a small Zapotec community with problems of access in the United States. Interestingly, television stations in more than seventy countries purchased the film.

Although the work documented in *No Access to Law* was basically ethnographically horizontal, a follow-up story about a single complaint introduced an innovative method. The examination of an American father's complaint to government agencies about why the synthetic material of a shirt worn by his son had burned so quickly, contributing to grave injury, generated a model of work that followed the history of a product, a history that involved regulatory agencies, manufacturers, and election monies during the Nixon presidency. The study of that one complaint documented a density of horizontal interaction at the top among the power holders in American politics and business to the exclusion of any significant vertical interaction between power holders and the victims of power transgressions. I refer to this model as "the vertical slice" (Nader, "Vertical Slice," 1980).

These different fieldwork experiences underscore a significant point: not only do different approaches yield new knowledge, but the knowledge so acquired works together to provide a manner of achieving understanding that is a distinct improvement on any single approach. Ethnography requires multiple approaches, in and out of the field. But it is the question that makes any methodology relevant in the first place.

OBSERVING LAWYERS AND LOCATING LEGAL HEGEMONIES

After my first three or four field experiences, I turned to a completely different set of experiences for insights into the meanings of something we in the West call "law." I began to read Michel Foucault and Antonio Gramsci on discourse and hegemony,
and Edward Said's work on how much of one's framing of the "other" is influenced by unquestioned assumptions in Western scholarship. I moved from notions of organization, agency, structure, and social relations to culture, specifically using the concepts of ideology and hegemony in reference to particular types of controlling processes. As a result of professional invitations, I began to interact with the American Bar Association at conferences. These conferences were in a sense fieldwork, although they were often brief engagements supplemented by library research and the following of legal policy debates in newspapers and journals. For example, in the 1960s, at a number of meetings between local bar groups and citizen groups, I found myself acting as translator for the two groups. Later, when invited to the National Judicial College in Reno, Nevada, I had the opportunity to observe judges who were, unbeknownst to them, participant observing in a jail cell. I watched them yelling, "Where's a chair, where's a goddamn chair?" The

purpose of this volatile (and now impermissible) experiment was to allow the judges to discover the connections between judicial action and its effects on the people who stand before judges for sentencing. The judges had not realized there were no chairs in jail. In the 1970s, conferences on law and development were also plentiful, as was optimism about tinkering with developing countries by means of legal transplants, an easy, fast, and cheap fix; a developing country need only buy a code book.

By the mid-1970s, complaints about access to law and about the inefficiencies of U.S. courts were so rampant that privileged solutions began to coalesce. In 1976 I was invited by the office of the chief justice of the U.S. Supreme Court to the Pound conference in St. Paul, Minnesota, a much-cited conference piggybacking on Dean Roscoe Pound's famous 1906 critique of the American justice system. As I have written elsewhere (Nader 1989), it was a rich experience, and somehow I do not believe that Dean Pound would have approved. Some of the pieces to the materials I had been puzzling over began to fit together. This conference was organized to discuss "a better way" to solve the problem of access to law. It was about how to distribute legal goods in response to social movement complaints about no access for civil rights, environmental rights, consumer rights, women's rights, native peoples' rights, and so forth. It was about the creation of new forums and, most certainly, about how to deal with the legal consequences of the social movements of the 1960s. It was also a conference for beleaguered judges, a venue for them to complain about their workplaces and the lack of support, financial and otherwise, that they had to endure.

The potential cases generated by the 1960s social movements

identified a new set of law users who had previously had little access to the courts. At the Pound conference these potential and real cases were referred to as the "garbage cases" (not an uncommon reference in legal policy circles), and it was argued that the courts should be reserved for the important cases. That there had to be "a better way" was the theme of Chief Justice Warren Burger at the conference and throughout the decade. That better way was alternative dispute resolution (ADR), a method for settling these new types of cases out of court in mediation sessions or possibly in arbitration. I was struck by the language the chief justice used and by the techniques he was using to convince the bar and the public that this alternative would relieve the American justice system of the overload coming in as a result of social activism. By the end of the conference, exhortation had clearly triumphed over reasoning, and rhetoric over substance: the new users of the court threatened the status quo. I began to outline a user theory of law.

A user theory of law (Nader 1985) stems from an assumption that the user, particularly the plaintiff user, is the driving force in law, not an abstraction like the courts or judicial decision. In this view, the direction of law depends mainly on what people are enabled and motivated to use the law to do. The trend toward a user theory of law emphasizes the role of the individual in molding social institutions. The drift of a legal system is thus prefigured by (among other things) use or non-use patterns that cumulate in a particular direction (Nader and Yngvesson 1974; Nader 1985). Law clearly comprises more than judicial or legislative institutions; it also includes the social and cultural organization of law.

By the time of the Pound conference, it was generally understood that law everywhere is variable within societies rather than constant. Cases between intimates are treated in one way, cases between strangers in another, and cases between people of unequal power in yet another. Yet, in some Middle Eastern villages and in the United States, the patterns of social control vary according to the social status of the parties involved in the dispute (Starr 1978; Yngvesson 1993). Among the Jalé of New Guinea, the social distance between the parties predicts the extent to which self-help operates within options ranging from dyadic conflict to war (Koch 1974). But the intent of ethnographies of law to describe and explain the processual models found within a society was to avoid the essentializing or caricaturing of societies that results from studying only the most salient or accessible means of disputing and to indicate the dynamic components in the life of the law. Within each society, patterned uses of disputing styles, such as penal, compensatory, therapeutic, and conciliatory, were part of the cultural analyses (Black 1976) in ethnographies of law, although not necessarily reported in four-fold tables.

Particular disputing processes were explained in terms of their own cultural attributes and their relationship to the culture and wider social forces that determine the number of available options. By the late 1970s, involvement in other activities had made me aware of the way in which local systems had to be thought of as open systems responding to the power structures of international order. In response to the idea that the nature of people's relationships imposes restraints on their settlement processes (Gluckman 1955), we challenged the notion that persons in multiplex relations adjudicate less. In disputes involving scarce resources, individuals may value the resources

more than they value social relationships, and they may be willing to sacrifice a social relationship with their opponent in order
to gain access to the contested resource (Starr and Yngvesson
1975). The disputants are active makers of the disputing process; different issues and not fixed relationships determine the
strategies disputants employ. Noncompromise outcomes commonly resulted from disputes over land or other important materials, or over access to power and influence within the community—all of which are, or are perceived as, scarce resources.
As I participated in international agencies and projects, I
learned the way in which colonial systems and, later, newly
independent countries, inspired by Western models of development, undercut local ideas of property and attempted to in-
troduce American ideas of law into other countries. When injustices became too great—as in Iran, where land rights were
revised—a revolution was provoked.

The concept of users as players in a dispute drama at the
microlevel is an interesting component in the macropicture because this concept looks at strategy in third-party decision making and challenges the assumption that the third party is neutral
or all-powerful. This concept is an important one also because
it overturns the previous picture of the passive plaintiff at the
mercy of a judge or jury and indicates the larger importance
of these social dramas. If we are to better understand the plaintiff role, the justice motive (Lerner 1975) must become central
to incorporating the perspective of all the parties to a case. Examining the interactions between people in disputes expands
the analytical framework within which process and power become indispensable variables. Users interact in broader processes by which they may become disempowered. The notion

of community law as being itself autonomous may be misleading in a globalized world in which various trading blocks may impinge on the very constitution of local life and, in the form of multinational institutions, change patterns of subsistence, order, and disorder. Throughout the years, the dominant schools of thought waxed and waned, but the general thrust was moving anthropological projects up and outward, away from a grounding in purely residential communities. Concern with differential power was building steam in the academy but not in the media or at professional conferences.

THE SELLING OF ADR

In the years after the Pound conference, the public became immersed in the rhetoric of ADR, a rhetoric in which language followed a restricted code and formulaics that combined clusters of meaning. My linguistic training was put to good use. ADR's proponents accomplished the pattern of assertive rhetoric by making broad generalizations, being repetitive, invoking authority and danger, and presenting values as facts. Because of his authoritative position as chief justice, Warren Burger set the tone for the language that characterized the speeches and writings of others, the tone for the selling of ADR. He warned that adversarial modes of conflict resolution were tearing the society apart. He claimed that Americans were inherently litigious, that alternative forums were more civilized than the courts; and the cold figures (meaning statistics) of the federal courts led him to conclude that we are the most litigious people on the globe. The framework of what I call coercive harmony began to take hold. Parallels were drawn between lawsuits and war, between arbitration and peace, parallels that invoked danger and suggested that litigation is not healthy (Nader 1989).

Although Burger's assertions were partial truths, his ADR movement could easily be construed as antilegal, a program for discouraging newcomers to the courts. He predicted that his better way, that is, ADR, would not take hold until the end of the century. Actually, however, it took hold and became institutionalized with such speed that many lawyers and social scientists were caught off guard. At this point in the work, I asked myself, was I doing ethnographic work when I was observing, participating, and writing about the Pound conference;[3] debating the seminal question What if *Brown v. Board of Education* had been mediated? at the 1999 American Bar Association meetings; zeroing in on African customary law at the meeting of American law schools in 2000; or explaining ADR to the National Association of Family Mediators some years earlier?

The questions became even more complex. After years of observing the ADR movement and its many ramifications, I had come full circle from the Zapotec research, which had concluded that harmony ideology was part of a pacification movement that originated with Christian missionaries and colonizers. Now I was observing another pacification movement that used the same tactics of "coercive harmony." Harmony law models placed new pulls on the American justice system, and attacks on the American tort system were ubiquitous. At the

---

3. Others have also published ethnographic descriptions of such conference experiences involving "the production, evaluation, dissemination, and collection of documents" (Riles 1998: 378).

same time, the ADR movement was going transnational. I sensed this from reading publications on international trade as well as observing Third World newcomers at conferences on "new" mediation techniques for Third World peoples. I began researching ADR as a soft technology of control, looking first at international river disputes (Nader 1995) and more recently at trade phenomena (Nader 1999). Though I might claim that I was participant observing at international conferences and international trade meetings, it was clear that in addition to meetings, library research had now become a key method for documenting the dissemination of a hegemony that had so quickly and so efficiently permeated a variety of institutions in the United States (schools, prisons, corporations, medical institutions) and that had then apparently moved out as part of the trend toward the Americanization of global law, which includes international law, as well as trade agreements, and more. In other words, the context for studying harmony law models was broadening to include transnational entities.

ZEROING IN ON POWER

Shifting the analysis of law toward its interactive elements meant that power differentials could not be ignored (Starr and Collier 1989). As anthropologists moved from the local arena into national and global spheres, where the social and physical distance between litigants was greater, disputing was increasingly recognized, as in the colonial setting, as occurring between strangers of unequal power. The self-conscious focus on power also underscored previous judgments that the case approach alone was not enough to sustain the analyses. Inequality often limited case action. State law, growing industrialization, and the separation of production from consumption have had as durable an effect on dispute resolution as did the change from nomadic to agricultural societies. Law in face-to-faceless societies that are characterized by highly unequal distributions of power does not always lend itself to the same solutions for handling disputes used in small face-to-face communities, where power differentials are more transparent. The study of law in face-to-faceless societies requires new, in addition to tried and true, methods for eliciting disputing profiles (Nader, *No Access,* 1980).

Paradoxically, ethnographic studies of law often remove law from the center of the study because in small-scale societies, where people share common social and political linkages (the sorts of places anthropologists have been apt to study), generalized social control rather than formal law results. In such settings, gossip and public opinion help deter socially harmful behavior and serve to direct disputes. Yet the more attentive we become to settings where formal written law or governmental control reigns, in places where the nation-state is fully developed, the more our studies center on the tension associated with hegemonic law and exclude other systems of law or control more generally. The traditional ethnographic studies of particular societies no longer suffice, although the ethnographic perspective is still being creatively applied to a dynamic understanding of law in complex societies, or what Bill Maurer (1996) recently referred to in the context of the Caribbean as the postmodern condition of creolization, transnationalism, and globalization. The anthropologist shifts the lens from bounded notions of social structure, family, and kinship to hybridity, globalization, and the movement of people and commodities across national borders.

Maurer worked in the British Virgin Islands (BVI), which is still a dependent colony of the United Kingdom, though it has its own laws and legislature. I found his ethnography especially interesting because when it was published, I was following the diffusion of ADR hegemony in local, national, and transnational settings. In his ethnography, Maurer was able to integrate many of the questions that I had thought about only in succession. He was doing something different from earlier ethnographies of law. He concentrated on the role of the state in the construction of BVI society and citizenship by means of law, exploring the paradox of a self-governing colony or dependency with its own laws and legislature. British common law, which is the foundation of BVI law and order identity, links up with the BVI legislature, which provides the basis for global financial offshore services. For Maurer, the distinction between law and custom is not always clear, because past legal practices become present customary practices, to the extent that the writing of BVI's national law has entrenched colonial rule and reinforced the world economy by creating a respectable tax haven for global financial markets. Furthermore, to compete for global capital, BVI revised its laws in 1990 so that tax havens became subject to outside monitoring, yet another paradox of increasing nationalism in an era of globalization. Maurer sees law and custom not as in opposition but as mutually constitutive, a point he makes in addressing the family-land issue; the crucial link between law and identity is the 1981 British Nationality Act, which, by limiting citizenship to legitimate children of citizens, made paternity central to legal and economic status. Maurer has moved a long way from the isolated indigenous community.

Before the postmodern period, some anthropologists looked at contemporary nation-states for legal phenomena functionally equivalent to those found in small-scale societies, phenomena such as negotiation, in order to examine social behavior such as cross-cultural negotiation (Gulliver 1979). Others looked for differences between traditional and modern settings, differences that had implications for evolutionary theory (Collier 1973; Moore 1986). Still others compared the management of economic grievances in face-to-faceless societies with the management of the same in the small, intimate face-to-face communities that for a century had been scrutinized by anthropologists (Nader, *No Access,* 1980). The search for an understanding of legal relations as they have changed over time, and particularly with the development of modern nation-states, is more a result of historical insight than of a dynamic concern with the contemporary period.

Perhaps both styles can be productive for insight and discovery. In my work, I have observed that the plaintiff role atrophies with the introduction of the nation-state because the state assumes the plaintiff role in criminal cases and the victim becomes the "real" plaintiff. Other anthropologists use a combination of approaches to investigate changes in culture that shape ideas about law and litigation quite independently of hegemonic forces, for the shaping of a perception of the law is itself a significant power gain for the civil society (Greenhouse 1986). We now are deeply interested in historicizing ethnography. Just as we innovated with the extended case method, situational analysis, social dramas, process, networks, actors, and meanings, we now move out of residential locales; and intellectual gains are the result.

Throughout my work, I developed and refined methodologies that suited the questions I was pursuing, but I do not think I could have accomplished much without that first intensive period of Zapotec fieldwork. In the 1960s, 1970s, and 1980s, I wrote several articles designed to expand thinking about methods in anthropology in particular and the social sciences more generally: "Perspectives Gained from Fieldwork" (1964a), "Up the Anthropologist" (1969b), "The Vertical Slice" (1980), and "Comparative Consciousness" (1994) among them. Although I valued the "how" of anthropology, the methods were not the purpose, only the means; they were subordinate to critical questions. Though I was not overly self-conscious about what I was doing, it became increasingly apparent that my essays were providing intellectual justification for pushing beyond the invisible boundaries of what was acceptable, what constituted the anthropology of law, and even beyond anthropology and ethnography, particularly in the more traditional sense of their being tied to a single locale and to acceptable methodologies such as participant observation. There were interesting questions that required more than participant observation.

In the 1970s, federal and state government in the United States, in concert with tribes and corporations, began to push for negotiated settlements in cases involving issues ranging from religious freedom and reparation to water, game, and fishing rights. Some years later, ADR entered the reservations via national Indian conferences, professional networks, and governmental and private institutions, the argument being that ADR was more compatible than litigating with "traditional" native culture and society. By the 1990s, I had spent about ten years researching and publishing on issues related to U.S. domestic energy practices, only to discover that ADR now took center stage in the struggle over nuclear waste storage on Indian lands (Nader and Ou 1998).

The study of indigenous law as it is affected by state and international power centers assumed major importance only recently. During the colonial period, law was created by clashes of interest between colonizers, and their missionizing activities, and the colonized. The method of control in Africa was indirect rule, in the United States, it was assimilation projects. Though the effects of foreign contact on "indigenous" law as shaped by the historical, social, and cultural features of the various societies seem obvious now, earlier anthropologists often seemed unaware of these effects.

In 1998, J. Ou and I discussed the current significance of a legal history that includes idealizing legal styles. The portrayal of self or of others is not benign, which is why representation became central to critical ethnographies. During the early days of the Red movement in the 1960s, Native Americans accepted the romantic vision of their culture as peaceful and harmonious, as able to compromise and search for win-win solutions. Such representations are part and parcel of the legal stratagems, sometimes bilateral, sometimes unilateral, that contending actors use to gain power. For example, federal bureaucrats make economic recommendations that are sold through a win-win discourse associated with the harmony legal model. Idealizations of Native Americans play an important part in legal power plays, especially those centering on the quest for scarce resources or those specific to environmental contamination.

It is axiomatic that barriers to thinking anew about an anthropology of "law" have to be removed by exoticizing what many thought was natural. If the study of the harmony law model, for example, leads us to a study of religious proselytizing, then that is where we should go. If an understanding of complaints leads us to moral minimalisms and the construction of suburbia, so be it. If the study of ADR takes us abroad and into the political economy of disputing and trade with China or Libya, that is where we should be. If an understanding of law, of why a young child's shirt burned so quickly, takes us into the Nixon White House to examine election bribery, that is where we should pursue the question. If customary law is being revived in Africa, history should inform us about the origins of "customary law" and its relation to law and development projects. And if a study of the nuclear waste problem takes us to negotiations on Indian reservations, that is where we should go.

LAW AND DEVELOPMENT

In Africa, colonization resulted in the creation of "customary law," which was later studied by anthropologists as if it were solely indigenous and relatively untouched by European peoples (Chanock 1985). Today, however, studies pay specific heed to state ownership and control of property, to technology transfer, and to the effects of demographic policies and policies that regulate natural resources, all of which involve analysis of external as well as internal processes. Such reappraisal was all part of

4. In the early 1980s, the Social Science Research Council's sponsored research on postcolonial appraisals was published in *Property, Social Struc-*

the reappraisal of anthropology that resulted from the demise of the colonial system and the rise of law and development projects, of which I was frequently a friendly critic.[4]

Arab countries have inherited legal systems from the colonial period that were heavily shaped by European legal systems. From the colonial experience there emerged a model of foreign intervention that used legal procedures as instruments of political and economic management, much in the way that the law and modernization movement uses such procedures today. Scholars point to the role of national law in emphasizing the continuity between colonial regimes and the new nations. This continuity of increased state power and of the centralizing power of the state through law is occurring in countries with social structures as different as those of Morocco, Tunisia, and Zambia. Whatever is perceived as threatening to the consolidation of the state, whether it be kinship alliances or landholdings or local control over water, is being undermined, sometimes gradually, sometimes drastically, by national law and also by supragovernmental institutions. Looking over these layers of inheritance, one gets a clear view of the various pathways Arab states followed toward centralized and Western-like legal systems, and why, beyond the fact that European systems offered greater control than did the decentralized systems of customary or Islamic courts.

In this respect, both historical documents and contemporary observation are useful in recognizing law as an agent of social and cultural change. In precolonial Tunisian oasis society, for

------

ture, and Law in the Middle East, edited by Ann Mayer with an introductory essay by Laura Nader (1985).

example, water ownership rather than land ownership formed the basis of power and prestige (Attia 1985). Water ownership, water distribution, and the management and upkeep of the intricate networks of canals and drainage ditches of the irrigation system required disciplined social organization. Transactions and work related to irrigation systems were regulated by customary law and managed by a hierarchical, castelike social structure of leading families and serfs tied to them in a quasi-feudal relationship. Changes in the concept of water as property accompanied the increased powers of the central government. The French colonial government's seizure of control of water management initiated the collapse of oasis society and the private ownership of water; and following independence, the Tunisian state continued the colonial pattern by abolishing private water ownership and use rights and bringing them under state ownership. State control of water ownership marked the ascendancy of the centralized government over regional power groups and, by means of the courts, destroyed the traditional rights of ownership and management of water. Thus, the transfer of water wealth among social groups was linked to the development of capitalist structures of production, which opened the door to transnational companies and the advent of neocolonialism.

In North Africa, colonizers regarded law as a fundamental tool in the appropriation and reorganization of land tenure (Leveau 1985). In Algeria, colonizers not only expropriated land by law but also dismissed the traditional inalienable character of land property in order to create a fluid land market. As a result of these legal measures, the Algerian social structure was deeply affected by the superimposition of individual property rights upon the previous collective property, a superimposition that is happening worldwide. The colonial methods applied in Algeria were also tried in Tunisia, the result was the expansion of the French administration. Gradually, by regarding natural resources such as land and water as legally independent from each other, the colonial state appropriated resources that were intimately linked to land. In this manner, Algerians were left with rights of use over only those natural resources that they had previously owned. Moreover, cooperative relationships between the colonizers and the Algerian bourgeoisie with regard to land issues heightened internal social inequalities that increasingly proletarianized peasants and tribes.

The use of law as a political instrument was not, of course, restricted to the colonial era. In the 1960s (the "development decade"), as colonialism was being dismantled in many parts of the world and as the Cold War was warming up, American lawyers were sent to Costa Rica, Brazil, Chile, Colombia, and Peru to extend legal assistance to the so-called Third World. "Legal aid" projects previously tested in countries such as India, Burma, and Japan and on the African continent were complementary to development projects sponsored by large United States developmental agencies preoccupied with the expansion of communism in the Third World. Most of the lawyers involved took with them idealized images of democratic law that clashed with the contrasting social, economic, and cultural features, for instance, of Latin American countries, most of which were not democratic. Nevertheless, the transfer of American legal models to these countries succeeded with respect to the American method of teaching law, the model of pragmatic lawyers, and the idea of law as instrumental (Gardner 1980). Those who benefited initially from this transfer were the lawyers and the elites, although populist legal reform movements in Brazil, for example, are ongoing.

Legal engineering was envisioned as a tool for social engineering. One aim was to further business transactions in liberal economies, an aim that presupposed predictable legal practices. Politically, such legal engineering was assessed as essential in the nation-building process and the spread of democratic institutions. Agencies such as the Ford Foundation, the United States Agency for International Development (USAID), and the International Legal Center provided millions of dollars to implement this project of legal engineering, and prestigious lawyers from private and public American universities as well as many authorities from diverse public institutions contributed to the design of the project. Owing to their vertical perspective on development and their blind overenthusiasm, which often failed to take into account the culture of the "receiver societies," the project took on an imperialistic character. Knowledge of local contexts is deemed relatively unnecessary if the goal is to remodel Third and Fourth World societies in the image of developed societies. Anthropologists were learning from historians and sociologists how colonialism had worked on "law."

The fact that social inequalities within these countries often stem from their subaltern position in relation to "core" countries was often ignored by underlying ideas of law and development as models to be imitated by Third World countries. This is apparent in various development projects funded by United States foreign assistance in the Middle East (Johnson and Lintner 1985). The Egyptian-American Rural Improvement Service (EARIS), the Jordan Valley Development Program, and the

Rahad Irrigation Project in Sudan, implemented from the early 1950s to the early 1980s, were undertaken to foster agricultural productivity. The underlying assumption of all three projects —

an assumption apparently shared by development lawyers (e.g., Zorn 1990)—was that poverty was the consequence of lack of technology and, therefore, that technological innovation would guarantee the alleviation of poverty.

Given that these projects apparently sought to improve the welfare of rural inhabitants, one would expect them to affect local organizing structures. One aim of the projects was to create new communities and to promote resettlement in Sudan and Egypt, as well as to incorporate Palestinian refugees in Jordan. Developers designed new cities but later abandoned them when it became obvious that they lacked traditional institutions like village councils or family networks. Agricultural innovation that depended on water supply from dams affected fishing rights. Land reform applied in the Jordan Valley altered traditional property through land distribution, appropriation of mineral rights by the state, centralized control over water, overlapping legal jurisdictions, and so on. In Sudan, the Rahan Irrigation Project reduced the grazing lands that nomadic herdsmen used for their livestock. Furthermore, because the reformers overlooked the ethnic component of the areas assigned to the projects, their legal engineering often exacerbated local tensions. Development engineers were learning from anthropologists.

The creation of new institutions under the auspices of development projects also challenged the traditional system of dispute settlements. In Swaziland, where Laurel Rose worked in

1992, the development forces refused to grant centrality either to "tradition" or to traditional chief-made law and instead used state law to justify their own notions of the primacy of individual property ownership over communal ownership as part of the economic and legal modernization project. In recognizing only national law, development projects failed to assess the legitimacy and operation of a multiplicity of legal systems that often competed or overlapped with state systems. Local groups became more tied to the state than they had been before through the imposition of new authorities and forms of social control. In the final analysis, however, these projects altered the coexisting foundations of religious law, customary law, and local law. Research on "customary law" illustrates that legal tradition is not petrified history; rather, legal tradition is constantly being invented. Anthropologists who have long worked with pluralistic or competing models (see, e.g., Mauss and Beuchat 1906 or later expositions by Pospisil [1971], Parnell [1988], and Merry [1988]) recognize that multiple models commonly evolve together and are rarely equal in power. Research on law and state power illustrates that, far from being neutral, law is often politically active, created by and for groups in power (Barnes 1961). This realization often separates anthropologists from development lawyers, who even today may still believe that "the rule of law" creates a level playing field that works out in practice.[5]

Once again, the methods should ideally be subordinate to the questions being pursued. Methods become eclectic because

5. This belief was reiterated more than once at the May 2000 conference on law and development at the University of Sussex in England.

loyalty to a single technique, even something like participant observation, commonly stultifies research. In addition, the domain of law itself needs to be recognized as artificial, as a defect in sociological studies that unnecessarily bound their domain. Indigenous systems of law that were described ethnographically as part of the indigenous culture and society are no longer described as closed systems. We have shifted our entire perspective on what constitutes indigenous culture and society, so that in the year 2002 we include legal transplants, missionary justice, USAID programs, and economic globalization as part of the local ethnographic picture, and once again anthropologists show their discomfort with drawing boundaries.

GLOBAL SYSTEMS
AND HEGEMONIC THEORY

In the decades when anthropologists were refining their ethnographic techniques, the concentration on particularities pushed comparison, diffusion, and time to the margin. Comparison became part of the internal analysis of variations, while cross-cultural comparison, developed at Yale by George Peter Murdock, was considered fraught with methodological difficulties, especially boundary questions, and therefore best avoided. The longitudinal method had seldom been used in ethnographies of law based on particular peoples. Llewellyn and Hoebel (1941) considered cases spanning a seventy-year period in Cheyenne history, but they compressed them into an ethnographic present and ignored external forces of change such as subjugation of these people by the U.S. government.

By the 1980s, ethnographers had developed ethnohistorical models of law that combined history and ethnography within the framework of power structures. Added consciousness about the position of the ethnographer in relation to his or her informants and the work of world systems theorists led to the examination of external forces or macrostructures on traditional microstructures. Anthropologists still consistently underestimate the extent to which Western political and religious traditions structure the control aspects of law. This underestimation is all the more surprising given the role of law in the areas where we have traditionally worked. Not only is law central to the so-called civilizing process, it is also an avenue for creating culture and a vehicle for its transmission.

By virtue of the background of the analysts and their entrapment in culturally constructed and disciplinary preferred models, theoretical discussions of styles of law obscure how value laden the models are. Although researchers now more often acknowledge and examine the ideological components underlying their own studies of law, certain ambiguities reveal that studies of legal systems carry a cultural load, such as a preference for harmony legal models over conflict-based ones, or for book law over traditional law. Enamored by the prospect of harmonious natives, anthropologists may in the past have exaggerated the argument that disputants with multiplex ties will try to compromise on their differences, just as many development lawyers are doing in the present. Such idealization may be used in surprising ways, ways not envisioned by those who embody them.

Anthropologists are alert to built-in biases. Scientific observers may be trapped by the thought systems of their own cultures, but they use different disciplinary lenses to screen data. The encounters between subordinate local political entities and dominant superordinate political entities did not immediately lead anthropologists to situate their studies of local law in the context of transplanted European legal, religious, and economic global systems. Although throughout the past century, we tended to leave the Europeans colonizers out of the analysis, recent work in legal history (Chanock 1985) and ethnography has begun to utilize both history and comparison to illuminate global interactive processes that shape local law (Moore 1986; Nader 1990).

EVERYONE WANTS
TO BE AN ANTHROPOLOGIST,
BUT IT'S NOT THAT EASY

In some ways the research trajectory of an anthropologist expands after the first long period of fieldwork. The work that follows is often not ethnography in the traditional sense but research that, though it moves beyond prolonged face-to-face research, is in many ways dependent on the researcher's having had a long period of study and residence in a well-defined place. It involves face-to-face engagements, knowledge of the language, participation in some of the observed activities, and an emphasis on intensive work with people rather than on survey data (which anthropologists may use as well). "Background issues" are frequently critical to the ethnographic thrust. Our traditional research techniques have been expanded by the use of tape recorders, film, and geologic surveys for mapping, but many ethnographers still go out in the field and stay for a long time. Writing anthropology about people as they are observed in their "natural habitat," some anthropologists describe ethnography as a craft that requires contextual specification and that seriously addresses the cultural translation problem in the final write-up of a book-length monograph.

Over the past twenty years or so, it has become fashionable to "do ethnography," as Arthur Kleinman pointed out in another context, however "lite" it may be. However, he adds that much of what is written discloses the writers' lack of serious training in ethnographic research. Ethnography, he emphasizes, is

> an anachronistic methodology in an era of extreme space-time compression.. . .it is seriously inefficient. In an era. . . witnessing the hegemony of analyses based in economic, molecular biological engineering. . .ethnography is not something one picks up in a weekend retreat.. . .it requires systematic training in anthropology. . .including mastery of ethnographic writing and social theory. . .and that, too, takes time. (1999, 76–88)

The attraction of the ethnographic method lies in its ability to come to terms with ramifications that bring with them unexpected moments of enlightenment.

For all the reasons that Kleinman proposes, the basic tenets of anthropological work need reiteration. We are presently working in an era of interdisciplinary and antidisciplinary moves, and as most readers know, disciplinary transgression is both a blessing and a curse; it can lead to repetition, imaginative thrust, or new knowledge. At this turn of the century, law is of critical importance to anthropology because of law's central role in transmitting hegemonies. At the same time, interdisciplinary work may result in decontextualized and dehydrated borrowings from anthropology by researchers trained in other fields. The recent focus on law and everyday life, for example, is posed as a discovery, when indeed what is being reaffirmed is the direction of the anthropological study of law over the past seven or eight decades. If what we wish to encourage is thick understandings of law *in* everyday life, it might behoove us to comprehend what anthropology of law has meant in different historical periods. Some of the skills gained in studying local communities may transfer to new contexts, contexts in which lawyers may be our most intellectually compatible colleagues. Though much has been written about the dark side of law as a tool for domination, the lighter side of law projects possibilities for democratic empowerment. The life of the law is the plaintiff, who, perhaps unwittingly, makes modern history, whether it be in small democracies found in local communities,

TWO

Lawyers and Anthropologists

The collision of force with opposing force is what sheds flying
sparks of illumination. That is why the ideal is habitually set off
against the positive, identity against time, the free against the
determined, reason against passion.. . .we need only call up the
fundamental classic antitheses of legal theory. . .Justice and Power,
Freedom and Order, Security and Change.

Edmond Cahn

Although this chapter is about lawyers and anthropologists, I
have never sought to make an interdisciplinary field out of law
and anthropology (although my work is informed by other disciplines), nor have I hoped to amalgamate the work of lawyers
and anthropologists (although we inform each other's work).
Indeed, I am skeptical, if not contemptuous, of lawyers who
claim the title of anthropologist merely because they are studying the law of everyday life or native peoples; they may find
the experience stimulating, but they have little grasp of what
ethnographic work entails. I know of no anthropologists who
claim to be lawyers solely because law is their subject of study;

thus my current perspective on the contemporary cacophony in legal and anthropological scholarship on law and in society prompts me to argue for separate but equal arenas: we do different things. We have much to learn from each other, but if we try to do each other's work, the work suffers from our naïveté and inexperience. Hence, if I refer to our relationships *as if* our disciplines had separate and autonomous existences, even though they do not, I do so for the simple satisfaction of better comprehending what we share and what we have to teach each other by virtue of the distinctiveness of our respective disciplines, even when the lawyer and the anthropologist are one and the same person.

I also wish to recognize the key ground common to the legal and anthropological disciplines that I am about to discuss. Both disciplines originate in Western thought, in particular worldviews. Such worldviews, no matter how "developed," become especially trenchant when Western lawyers and Western anthropologists find themselves on foreign soil, where they are both, whether they realize it or not, representing distinct Euro-American interests in their relation to other cultures. A sort of Euro-American bias in anthropology—a romantic notion of indigenes' presumed relation to the law—was wonderfully apparent during a 1997 American Anthropology Association symposium on intellectual property. Participating anthropologists had gone to the field to study everything from tourism to identity, only to be reoriented by the issues central to indigenous people—national and international property law. Intellectual, cultural, and biological properties were endangered, and indigenes pulled both lawyers and anthropologists into their orbits.

One final point at the beginning of this chapter has to do with why the disciplines have come to intersect so frequently. Unlike lawyers and astronomers, or anthropologists and investment bankers, lawyers and anthropologists keep crossing paths: in the library, in the field, at development conferences, in political situations. Lawyers were among the first to contribute to the ethnology and ethnography of law in order to respond to inquiries about comparative law and the problems of cultural subjectivity. Both disciplines confront power in the relationships between subordinates and superordinates, and anthropology all the more, since "tradition" and law have commonly been used as political stratagems in colonial settings (Colson 1974). But, above all, our work overlaps in breadth and scope. Anthropologists and lawyers can be generalists. As the American jurist Oliver Wendell Holmes once put it, the law is "one big anthropological document" (1920: 212).

This second chapter illustrates the intersection between anthropology and law by reference to examples of the intersection or invention of the subject matter that has brought our two professions together over the last century. I have chosen these examples from research on law conducted (1) in the latter part of the nineteenth century in the United States, when European colonialism reigned worldwide and when the United States' takeover of Indian lands was being completed; (2) during the 1930s and 1940s in the United States, when industrialization had taken root, bringing with it immigration and prosperity, as well as economic depression; and (3) in the United States and England over the past twenty-five years, during which time Euro-American hegemony peaked and confronted future decline.

This chapter contains the seeds of the two that follow: first, the value of the multiple lenses—comparative, historical, and ethnographic—generated by a succession of questions that required custom-made field and analytical methodologies and, second, the Euro-American controls inherent in hegemonic models in law that are discovered by firsthand experiences in the field. Throughout this chapter, the increasing importance of the civil plaintiff becomes plain in a law that since the rise of the nation-state has overall been less than hospitable to the plaintiff. But I am getting ahead of my story, in which for me the sociology of knowledge plays an important part.

The dynamics of law study had its beginnings in the nineteenth century, when anthropology was still forming as a discipline. Law, on the other hand, had had disciplinary status for centuries. Scholars who figure in the nineteenth-century were independent thinkers, lawyers and anthropologists who, it has been said, pulled the bottom out of history, a history previously dominated by biblical origins, and who fearlessly addressed the large-scale issues of their times. Those who first investigated the difference between Western and non-Western law were largely armchair intellectuals, but they nevertheless collected enough data to begin to document differences; law was stratified variously by some into stages like savagery, barbarism, and civilization—stages that are still found in Western thought processes and law and development schemes.

In the first six decades of the twentieth century, field ethnographers made significant headway in the understanding of law in particular societies, starting from the premise that those societies were discrete units. Although an interest in particular societies may have been in part a reaction to the grand armchair theorists of the nineteenth century, the premise that societies were self-contained and set apart was also to produce a coun-terreaction. With the shrinking universe before us, and with the continuing diffusion and reuse of Western legal ideas in colonies and former colonies, anthropologists and legal scholars now move beyond the particular to examine the larger patterns of change that have in part resulted from Western economic expansion and the rise of East Asian economies.

THE NINETEENTH-CENTURY DEBATES

The nineteenth century provides us with numerous distin-guished lawyers—among them Sir Henry Maine, an English-man; Lewis Henry Morgan, an American; J. F. McLennan, a Scotsman; and Johann Bachofen, from Switzerland—who worked with historical and comparative methods to develop a science of society. Although Morgan was the only one among them who was also a firsthand observer of indigenous peoples, there is hardly a history of anthropology that does not count these figures as forerunners in the field, while always, of course, making reference to but not including Freidrich Karl von Sa-vigny, the Germanic historical school of jurisprudence, and the Italian scholar Giambattista Vico. The nineteenth century was a turbulent period, a period when divisions between lawyers and anthropologists, between advocacy and objectivity, and be-tween reform-minded and ivory tower scholarship had not yet been established.[1] These were men who used their scholarship

1. See Mary Furner's *Advocacy and Objectivity: A Crisis in the Profes-sionalization of American Social Science, 1985–1905* (1975). She devotes

as a means to understand their changing political present and the global impact of industrialization. It was a time when lawyers were among the leading anthropologists, when lawyers were scholars who used historical and evolutionary schools of thought to make sense of their world. Both schools—historical and evolutionary—were controversial; both created uncomfortable reactions among their wide-ranging publics.

In 1861, Sir Henry Maine examined historical materials from Europe and India, arguing that changing relations in law, notably the transition in emphasis from status to contract, were a result of societal shifts from kinship-based communities to territorially organized nations. Those who followed Maine contended that in accordance with dominant modes of subsistence, human societies were scaled along a progressive sequence of legal systems that developed gradually from self-help to penal or compensatory sanctions associated with government law.

According to Maine's biographer, the historical school was an irritant, especially as it was portrayed by Maine. Its social critics attacked the comparative historical methodology: "A hundred years ago people used to ask whether a thing was true; now they only want to know how it came to pass for true." The same critics referred to the "abuse of a method which in the hands of Maine and others had been producing such dazzling results." Others spoke of a "joint-stock-mutual-puff-and-

_____

much attention to economics in the 1880s, a decade when first-generation professionals wrestled with the social questions associated with industrialism.

admiration society" (Feaver 1969: 137). It is not surprising that there was contention. The nineteenth century was a time when the laboring class was pitted against the capitalists, the aristocrats were pitted against the more democratically inclined, religion was pitted against science, and older histories with short chronologies were pitted against newer ones with chronologies stretching into prehistory.

Sir Henry Maine's "academic conservatism" was concerned with the old and the new, with the undesirability of democracies when stripped of their emotional appeal. He compared democracies with an aristocracy of intellect as the political ideal, an ideal, an aristocracy, in which there would be no scope for demagogues to challenge the future of British imperial hegemony and British domestic policies. Maine was striving for a social history:

> We of western Europe might come to understand ourselves better. We are perhaps too apt to consider ourselves as exclusively children of the age of free trade and scientific discovery. But most of the elements of human society, like most of that which goes to make an individual man, comes by inheritance. It is true that the old order changes, yielding place to new, but the new does not wholly consist of positive additions to the old; much of it is merely the old very slightly modified, very slightly displaced, and very superficially recombined. (Feaver 1969: 152)

Across the waters in the United States, Lewis Henry Morgan also had his political concerns, although his were with democracy, not aristocracy, and with evolutionary, not historical, theory. Again the biographers describe the historical context for debate. The concerns of Morgan the Whig did not always concur with those of Maine the Tory. Morgan, a lawyer for business investors in railroads and minerals in Michigan, was caught up with his contemporaries in the task of delineating the gulf between the civilized and the uncivilized. Native Americans were to be admired. After all, the polity of the Iroquois Confederacy had inspired Morgan's position on the relative importance of democracy over property: "Democracy in government, brotherhood in society, equality in rights and privileges, and universal education, foreshadow the next higher plane of society to which intelligence and knowledge are steadily tending" (Feaver 1969: 163). Yet many thought of the Iroquois as savages, as uncultured and un-Christian.

In his studies of Native American social organization, Morgan's analytical categories came from law, his theories from evolutionary thought. Following Sir William Blackstone (1897), Morgan recognized Iroquois laws of descent by contrast; they followed the female line. Morgan used a lawyer's form to understand the league of the Iroquois, the confederacy of the Six Nations that was their polity. He examined American Indian treaties and advocated for native peoples while at the same time recognizing the savage intellectual who, as he put it, created a system of wonderful complexity. He concluded that inequality was social rather than innate (Resek 1960: 52). For Morgan, "economic man was a transient in history." By contrast, Maine had argued in his Rede lecture, "Nobody is at liberty to attack several property and to say at the same time he values civilization" (Feaver 1969: 163). The two men were locked in opposing camps.

From firsthand experience, Morgan understood the significance of the transformation of communal property into private property in the American West. He was witness to the granting of public lands to railroads, and his biographer, C. Resek (1960: 104), comments: "In regions where Indian tribes once roamed freely, a civilized government claimed, then distributed natural resources, and finally sanctioned their private ownership. The quest for property in Upper Michigan had destroyed tribal life, brought on corporative wars, and produced marked changes in Morgan's character. Property was obviously a powerful force in human relations." Morgan's firsthand observations about property were not limited to Native Americans. Resek, quoting from Morgan's *Journal of a European Trip, 1870–1871,* reports that Morgan had only scorn for the conditions in Europe because of the extremes of poverty and wealth: "The aristocracy ride and the people carry them by their industry.. . .the poor were defrauded of their just rights before they were born" (122). Morgan was an intellectual and an activist; though offered the opportunity to be a professor, he did not think he had the disposition. He ran for the New York State Senate not because he wanted to be a politician but because he wanted to be (but never was) commissioner of Indian affairs. For him, there were wrongs to be righted.

Theoretical differences between Maine and Morgan stem most obviously from Morgan's familiarity with Native American peoples and from his observations about the notions of descent and property, observations based on original fieldwork among a group that was organized along matrilineal principles. Maine was concerned with "ancient communities" as they impinged on his contemporary world, which was organized along patrilineal principles. The year after publication of his *Ancient Law* (1861), he joined the colonial establishment in India as legal member of the Supreme Council of the Governor-General, and later he became vice chancellor of the University of Calcutta. He was never interested in "savages," and when he writes to Morgan, he refers to himself as a "Professor of Jurisprudence" and makes disparaging reference to the "anthropologists."

Morgan apparently had a nervous disposition; Maine, as described by Robert Lowie (1937: 50), was "the embodiment of serene wisdom coupled with unusual subtlety." He was an armchair anthropologist who, disregarding the disparities in wealth in the English countryside, dedicated himself to comparing Roman law and contemporary Western legal systems with early Indo-Germanic law. Ethnography influenced only a very small part of his thinking. He was a historian dealing with "the real" as opposed to an evolutionist making speculative use of ethnographies. In his *Ancient Law,* Maine treated law as inseparable from kinship, religion, and morality. A historical functionalist, he has a place in history that is justified by the fact that he enlarged the scope of comparative law and clarified such concepts as tort and crime, status and contract. He took issue particularly with Morgan's theories of matrilineal descent, which he felt were "repugnant to basic facts of human nature" and the idea of patrilineal authority based on the sheer physical superiority of the male of the species (Feaver 1969: 167). To say mother right came before father right was to challenge the patri-monogamous family as an essential part of the evolutionary models that stipulated set stages of transformation.

Imagine the scene: Two nineteenth-century schools of thought about matriarchy and patriarchy promulgated by male lawyers, in an age when equality and its opposite were burning issues. Morgan, the upstart American, described a striking form of descent in which children were assigned to the mother's tribe and in which property, titles, and offices were passed through the matriline; the son did not succeed the office of the father and did not inherit his father's property, only his mother's. In a society dominated by Victorian male household heads, assertions that women had once been the politically powerful sex appeared to be wild-headed, free-for-all, sloppy scholarship. Morgan staunchly defended his views and even invited Maine to come to the United States to see for himself. Today we recognize the existence of different lines of descent, but in the first half of the nineteenth century, what was thought possible was intimately connected to subjective experience. Particularly with regard to the history of property, Maine turned to India for corroboration, Morgan to the Native American peoples among whom he lived and traveled.

Disagreement was plentiful between these and other lawyer-anthropologists. McLennan the Scotsman, Bachofen the Swiss, and Maine the Englishman, for example, were heralding widely divergent views on the legal position of women. Maine took the position that women "had had no individual personality in early times, and that while similar conditions continued to prevail in Western progressive societies there had been a constant widening of the personal and proprietary liberty of women"; in contemporary India, he noted, the wife remained bound to the legal personality of her husband (Feaver 1969: 142–43). Maine's position was in direct opposition to Bachofen and McLennan's theses of early matriarchal ascendancy.

Several recent critiques in anthropology underscore the degree to which Maine's immersion in the ideas and assumptions of his own culture led him to conclusions about the progressive evolution of legal forms, conclusions that were not supported by the facts (Kuper 1985; Starr 1989). June Starr, an anthropologist and lawyer who has studied the status of upper-class Roman women as it related to their ability to control property, scrutinizes Maine's use of this data in his *Ancient Law.* She concludes: "Females were not free of paternal and male guardianship. They did not have control of their property or even their own persons in the second century A.D. as Maine had asserted.. . .Although Maine shifted his positions later, in *Ancient Law,* he had stated: 'Ancient law subordinates the woman to her blood-relatives, while a prime phenomenon of modern jurisprudence has been her subordination to her husband'" (Starr 1989: 357). Starr goes on to point out that "much of the impetus for women to gain voting rights in Great Britain and the United States in fact grew out of the laws that restricted married women from controlling their inherited property" (358). She goes to the trouble of correcting Maine's conclusions for her anthropological audience because she (as well as Kuper) believes that his hold on anthropologists is still strong. Refuting Morgan's description of Iroquois social organization would be much more difficult, although his evolutionary scheme has been attacked by anthropologists more severely than has Maine's progressive evolution of legal forms.

What is of interest today is the persistence of the male bias that led to erroneous conclusions in Sir Henry Maine's work. In their excellent work titled *Women and Colonization,* editors Etienne and Leacock (1980) point out that the Victorians looked upon women in non-Western societies as oppressed and servile beings who would eventually be liberated by attaining a progressive, civilized life. In twentieth-century anthropology, this same male bias, if in a more sophisticated version, still prevailed, not only among distinguished male anthropologists such as E. E. Evans-Pritchard and Claude Lévi-Strauss (Etienne and Leacock 1980: 1–3) but also among some feminist anthropologists, such as Sherry Ortner and Michele Rosaldo (1–5). A paper on the Seneca by Diane Rothenberg in this same 1980 collection shows how male bias (including Morgan's) has led to misinterpretation of the relation between the sexes and the meaning of the observation that the land "belonged" to the women.

Today the issues sound familiar: the nature of nature, the nature of progress, the role of political democracy in the absence of economic democracy. For Maine and Bachofen, democracy was repugnant; for Morgan and McLennan, it was an inspiration. But it is clear in reading nineteenth-century work, especially the ethnographic work, that they all considered progressivism a creed (as it is considered today), whether it came about by legal reform (Maine) or material betterment (Morgan). The ethnologizing of the past was linked to their legal anthropologies as well as to their visions of the future. In all cases, the veracity of history was at stake; so too was what Bachofen called "cultural subjectivity." New worlds were opening up, world conditions were rapidly changing, and ethnocentrism was (and remains) deeply entrenched.

FIELDWORK AND REALISM

In the early twentieth century, two of anthropology's distinguished scholars were engaged in debate about the boundaries and meaning of law. By 1926, Bronislaw Malinowski had broken with past armchair methods and used firsthand ethnographic field observations to destroy widespread myths about law and order among preliterate peoples. His work on the connection between social control and social relations foreshadowed a generation of anthropological research on how order could be achieved in societies lacking central authority, codes, and constables. He pushed the boundaries of law to include more than the formal or informal rules and restrictions; for example, he included theories of reciprocity, exchange, or binding obligations. Malinowski's contemporary, A. R. Radcliffe-Brown, instead used a jurisprudential approach, following Roscoe Pound's definition of law as "social control through the systematic application of the force of politically organized society" (Radcliffe-Brown 1933: 202). Radcliffe-Brown's approach, which defined law in terms of organized legal sanctions and concluded that some "simpler" societies had no law, had very little impact on the ethnographies of future generations of anthropologists studying stateless societies.

For a while, the question of whether all societies had law was hotly debated. If law is defined in terms of politically organized authority, as Radcliffe-Brown and his adherents would have it, then not all societies can be said to have law. Only those societies that have created legal institutions of government such as courts and constables have law. But if—following Malinowski—law is defined as the processes of social control by which any society maintains order and discourages disorder, then all societies can be said to have law, and social control becomes more or less synonymous with law. Under this definition, all societies can be said to be "civilized." Once again, the conflict is between hierarchy and more egalitarian democratic relationships.

The debate over the boundaries and meaning of law is, of course, an old one in other disciplines too. In political theory, for example, one tradition identifies the laws of a society as the minimal rules of conduct acknowledged by the members of that society, whereas the opposing tradition identifies the laws of a society as the formal commands of the governing authority of that society. Thus, Locke posits that there is law in primitive societies, and Hobbes argues that there is no law without a state political organization. Marxian theory takes a divided stand on this question. More recently, legal realist Karl Llewellyn was passionately against narrowing the field of law. As he stated his position: "So I am not going to attempt a definition of law.... A definition both expands and includes...and the exclusion is almost always rather arbitrary. I have no desire to exclude anything from matters legal. In one aspect law is as broad as life" (Twining 1973: 591). But anthropological field-workers soon moved beyond the issue of definition and contributed to an understanding of this question by extending our knowledge of human variation and sociocultural transformations. Today most anthropologists of law do not define law in any narrow way, although they may speak of universal attributes of law (Pospisil 1958). Nor do they attempt to impose on their data Western distinctions such as those between crime, tort, delict, sin, and immorality. In line with the argument over the culture-boundedness of Western jurisprudential categories, few anthropologists apply the private/public distinction cross-culturally. Instead, ethnographers adopt, for purposes of analysis, the analytical or folk categories of preferred theories (Bohannan 1957). And so it was with *The Cheyenne Way*.

In 1941, when many Americans were still reeling from the effects of the 1929 stock market crash and the violence and conflict that had erupted on the European and Pacific stages, people were thinking about wars to end all wars, about how to make a better world, and about how to make laws fit with the fast-changing realities of mass production and mass consumption. That year marked the publication of *The Cheyenne Way: Conflict and Case Law in Primitive Jurisprudence* by Karl Nickerson Llewellyn, a Yale-trained, flamboyant, and crusading professor of law at Columbia University, and E. Adamson Hoebel, a modest professor of anthropology. Together the two scholars, one a leader in the school of legal realism, the other influenced by the relativist and functionalist schools of anthropology, began a new inquiry into law and its relation to culture and society. Their theory of law was based primarily on lawbreaking. Their book is an excellent introduction to the more-general thought processes of Karl Llewellyn, processes tempered by the Cheyenne and stimulated by the political and economic ferment of the 1930s in the United States.

The Cheyenne Way was an achievement of cooperation between a distinguished law professor who admired the craft of law practice and who emphasized the investigation of trouble-cases, and a seasoned anthropologist for whom trouble-cases were central to the analysis of law in its cultural context. The endeavor was extraordinary because the setting for Llewellyn and Hoebel's investigation was among an American Indian people and because an explicit purpose of their cultural analysis was to subject Western ideas about law to comparative scrutiny.

The Cheyenne had originally inhabited the woodland lake country of the upper Mississippi Valley and were among the westernmost speakers of the Algonkin languages. By the beginning of the nineteenth century, and as a result of the often violent contact between the Cheyenne and European and American culture and the United States government, the Cheyenne had adopted a new economy based on horse culture and buffalo hunting. It was an economy that caught white people's imagination. Although Llewellyn and Hoebel were not the first to study the Cheyenne, they thought it necessary to supplement the published data on the Cheyenne with their own fieldwork among the northern Cheyenne of the Tongue River Reservation at Lame Deer, Montana. They worked together during the summer of 1935; the following summer Hoebel returned to Montana for additional materials. But *The Cheyenne Way* does not set out to present a full outline of the history and culture of the Cheyenne. Rather, it focused on comparing modern and primitive law.

By the time Llewellyn arrived in New Haven as a student, William Graham Sumner had already had a long career at Yale. Sumner's political sociology had incorporated the comparative method of European anthropologists and ethnographers. Sumner also recognized the all-important function of extralegal methods of social control. His *Folkways* (1907) was widely read, and his ideas about ethnocentrism and his critique of belief in the superiority of one's own society to that of others were having impact. For Llewellyn, folkways (the current ways of doing things in a society to satisfy human needs or desires) became law-ways, and he came to share Sumner's firm conviction that ethnography should be preeminent as the "data" and substance of social analysis. At Yale Law School Llewellyn came into contact with the early exponents of what would later be called legal realism: W. N. Hohfield, W. W. Cook, and A. L. Corbin. Legal realism was a challenge to the formalism of Christopher Columbus Langdell, who had become dean of Harvard Law School in 1870 with a mandate from the president of Harvard University to revolutionize the law school. Langdell's most far-reaching innovation was the introduction of the case method for teaching law. Langdell considered law a science that proceeded inductively, using cases as primary sources. The concepts and principles of law unfolded through a series of cases from which the genius of the common law was extracted. But only some cases were useful for his purpose; the majority of cases were useless and worse than useless for the purpose of systematic study.

Although the new Langdellian method had its value, legal realists criticized it for severing the ties between the study of law, American scholarship, and everyday life. The method was, by its formality, strictly segregated from scholarly life. The formal style stressed order and logic in the law. At the beginning of *The Common Law* (1881: 1), Oliver Wendell Holmes, a contemporary of Langdell, wrote that "the life of the law has not been logic, it has been experience." This statement was to become an identifying mark of the school of legal realists of the 1920s and 1930s.

Karl Llewellyn, Jerome Frank, and others battled against a jurisprudence of concepts and for one of experience (see Hull

1997). Legal realism sought to represent the whole by means of the parts, which were thought to evoke a cultural and social totality. The realist judges and writers had little tolerance for legal tradition for its own sake. Law had to be an all-around working tool that questioned the rules, the citations, the fictions, and the apparent rationalities stemming from deductive reasoning. The philosophy of Langdell, they argued, had no place in a dynamic American context. Dissent became a more common practice, prevailing over the United States Supreme Court's usually unanimous decisions. The realist movement brought law back into the world of intellectuals, into the scholarly life of a less specialized, narrow sort, and had some influence on law school curriculums. Not all were convinced by the realists, and for some it was an unreal realism, but the realist context helps explain why *The Cheyenne Way*—in spite of its extravagant style, its often involuted expression, and its lack of attention to the ethnographic literature—was so significant (Malinowski 1942: 1237, 1250).

The relationship between Llewellyn and Hoebel began in 1933, when Hoebel was a twenty-six-year-old graduate student in anthropology at Columbia University in New York. It was an exceptional time in anthropology. Franz Boas and Ruth Benedict were the leaders in the field, but neither was interested in Hoebel's idea of studying the law of the Plains Indians: since the Plains Indians had no well-defined government structures, why would they have something called "law"? Malinowski's widespread theories about the universality of law, long known to readers outside anthropology, had, it seemed, not yet penetrated the thinking of Columbia anthropologists. Karl Llewellyn was then Betts Professor of Jurisprudence at Columbia University Law School. At age forty, he was already a well-known advocate of the controversial school of legal realism. He had been exposed to sociology and anthropology while studying at Yale and abroad and had found in those disciplines ideas that were congenial to his legal realism program.

Llewellyn and Hoebel's work has been described by many as the most successful example of an interdisciplinary collaboration. According to William Twining's (1973) biography of Karl Llewellyn, Llewellyn spent only ten days in fieldwork among the Cheyenne, but it was he who contributed the basic theory and who was the source for the case-method approach. Hoebel was the field-worker, experienced in the culture of the Plains from earlier work with the Comanche and the Shoshone, and he collected the data for the ethnographic portions of the text. Thus the collaboration was a meeting of realistic jurisprudence and functional anthropology. Both Llewellyn and Hoebel were gifted writers with a knack for the poetic turn of phrase and the apt anecdote to portray cultural systems, but they had very different personalities. Llewellyn is often described as robust, contentious, vigorous. Hoebel is known for a more modest, composed style and his preference for order and harmony. Their differences made for good collaboration, but the engine was clearly Llewellyn's.

In *The Cheyenne Way,* Llewellyn and Hoebel devised a methodology for studying what was then called "tribal" law—the detailed study of actual disputes. For them, it was apparent that where there are no books, there is only law in action. The work was based on the law-jobs theory, a harmonious juristic model, which posits that in all human societies, group survival and cooperative activity depend on the satisfactory settlement of dispute or on its prevention.

The Cheyenne Way differed from Llewellyn and Hoebel's later collaboration on the law-ways of the Keresan Pueblos of the Southwest. The aims of that investigation, which was undertaken by invitation of the special attorney for the United Pueblos Agency, were to be practical. The recording of Keresan Pueblo law would support its continuance and defend it against those who would question and destroy traditional ways. The very act of recording and publishing Pueblo law would *supposedly* protect the people's autonomy.

Llewellyn became especially interested in the contradictions of the Pueblo experience, which combines theocratic, communal, and totalitarian features. As he stated, he wanted to investigate

> the relation of religious freedom to a Church-State Unity and the problems of toleration, tolerance, and repression of dissenting views.. . .Or the problem of maintaining or adjusting an ingrained ideology without disruption of its values, with a younger generation affected by a wider and utterly diverse ideology; and of producing peaceful relations with an utterly diverse neighboring, and to some extent predatory, culture. Or, the manner and degree in which officially unrecognized changes creep in under maintenance of the older ideology and forms. (Twining 1973: 568)

Hoebel had other interests, including his wish to test Ruth Benedict's tantalizing idea that the Pueblos had a system of social control enforced not by coercive physical sanctions but rather by an intense degree of personal internalization of norms of social cooperation (Hoebel 1969).

In *The Cheyenne Way,* Llewellyn and Hoebel's interests dovetailed more than they did in the Pueblos study, where Llewellyn was increasingly a practitioner, drafting codes and giving advice while Hoebel remained detached and, some say, less sympathetic to the Pueblos and less interested in Llewellyn's involvement in the practical aspects of the project. In discussing the partnership, Llewellyn's biographer put it this way:

> The success was due in part to common, in part to complementary, characteristics. Both men were interested in jurisprudential questions and this provided an identity of objectives, the absence of which is the first obstacle to this type of collaboration. Both favoured the closer integration of the social sciences. Temperamentally they were well suited: each had a touch of the poet....in other respects their characters were complementary, never more so than in the matter of obtaining a balance between imaginative insight and hard fact. Llewellyn's genius lay in devising new approaches, he was less fitted for applying them systematically. His inclination and aptitude for sustained fieldwork were limited. Hoebel, on the other hand, was both by training and temperament an excellent fieldworker... and he was prepared to accept the role of disciple of Llewellyn's theories....If Hoebel had been a rebel against Malinowski's functionalism, or if Llewellyn had been a more orthodox lawyer, collaboration would have been harder and much less fruitful. (Twining 1973: 568)

Llewellyn was a man with scope, a man who wanted a diverse playing field. Nothing less would allow him the wide angle needed for cultural critique, cultural improvement, or simply cultural illumination. A passage from the last chapter of *The Cheyenne Way* indicates what he and Hoebel had in mind: "What the Cheyenne law-way does for Americans...is to make clear that under ideal conditions the art and the job of combining long-range justice, existing law, and the justice of the individual case, in ways reasonably free of the deflecting pressures of politics and personal desire, need not be confined to the judging office. It can be learned elsewhere and learned rather generally" (Llewellyn and Hoebel 1941: 335). Realistic law was to be integrated into every aspect of society. Legal formalism, however, was a disintegrating force. Llewellyn was an uncompromising foe of such formalism, an advocate of a practical, experiential jurisprudence rather than an obscure or philosophical one. Collaboration with an anthropological fieldworker suited him perfectly, for without a written law, experience perforce became central.

Llewellyn had only a peripheral interest in the Cheyenne, and the ethnographic in general, but he recognized the primitive as a powerful frame within which to represent alternative possibilities for juridical planning to an American readership. If, on Llewellyn's side, the German romantics with their ideal of holism and the interweaving of all the parts into the whole were crucial to the realist's law, then the failure of the legal realists and the functionalist anthropologists of their day to see eye to eye was no surprise.

The point is that Llewellyn and Hoebel shared intellectual roots they might not have shared if Llewellyn had been a more orthodox lawyer of his time or if Hoebel had been a less broad-gauged social scientist. But they both had their blind spots. *The*

Cheyenne Way deals synchronically with the historical period between 1820 and 1880. In the cases Llewellyn and Hoebel considered, individual interests, particular personalities, and the general interests of the whole group lay behind the rules, both legal and nonlegal, used to arrive at solutions. Cheyenne dispute settlement resulted in the reordering of society. They attended to the law-jobs that any group faces in the process of becoming and remaining a group: multiple informal modes of control like those found in any society reinforced the law-ways and were used to "clean up social messes" (20)

The unrealism of this kind of functionalist realism stems from an inability to deal with Cheyenne law as an open system. Their book ignores the harsh realities of the effects on Cheyenne law of the white people's conquest and the decimation of the Cheyenne people through disease and forced migration. That the Cheyenne were left in turmoil by what, in the Pueblos context, Llewellyn willingly called a "neighboring predatory culture" is barely alluded to in *The Cheyenne Way*. Llewellyn and Hoebel were not interested in what genocide does to law-ways. Rather, in 1941, theirs was a sense of romance and discovery, an insight into Cheyenne culture as it bore on their own culture.

One can see both their romantic vision and their critical purpose in their comments on the pipe-procedure type of settlement:

> For if a law technique is to make its way without the aid
> of centralized will and force to drive it through, it must
> not only be effective socially, but must also make personal
> appeal.. . .The spread of a pattern of process—or rule—
> by growth and contagion, by what one may term the more

democratic processes, is quite another matter from its
spread by way of authority. One can match the delay in
the contagion of the superior Cheyenne technique of chief-
and-pipe with the nonsuccess or slow spread of many of
the finest pieces of case-law hit upon in the last half-
century by one or another of the multi-headed courts
among the United States. (47)

Trouble-cases, they believed, provided "the safest main road
into the discovery of law" (29).

The Cheyenne had no legal professionals and scarcely anything like fixed rules of law, but they were not automatons.
They could innovate and, under new circumstances, create new
law. They provided an example of the cultural malleability of
human institutions and by example showed that certainty and
form need not be sacrificed to achieve flexible justice. Solutions
to modern problems were to be found in other cultures.

The 1920s and 1930s appear now as a time of reassessing
dominant ideas and of borrowing across disciplines, and the
intellectual stimulus provided by this borrowing changed readership patterns. World War I, the 1929 stock market crash, and
the Great Depression that followed had caused uncertainty and
major changes not easily explained by existing theory about
social order. For students of American anthropologist Franz
Boas, cultural critique was grounded mostly in the study of
Native Americans, through whom writers could show that
there were different ways to order society that were at least as
rational as ours. Few fields in the 1920s and 1930s were untouched by the critical insight provided by this ethnographic
encounter with other peoples, an encounter that showed us a
way of better understanding our own culture.

In *The Cheyenne Way,* Llewellyn and Hoebel treated individual cases as emerging from problems that required solutions, the basic general task of handling trouble-cases being to maintain order. They rejected the idea of law as the sum total of abstract rules; besides, some societies use rules only sparingly: "The trouble-cases, sought out and examined with care, are thus the safest main road into the discovery of law. Their data are most certain. Their yield is richest. They are the most revealing" (29). But if trouble-cases define the norm, their value lies in the revelation of the command that prevails in the pinch. The notion of justice is key. Cases are not merely opportunities for the elaboration of doctrine; rather, laws are imperatives that stem from community life. The case method was a key to the law in motion: law emerges from the morality, decency, and good taste of a people. Law-ways are not set down as things apart; instead, they cling close to tribal life as it evolves.

Some scholars insist that the case method, with its focus on institutionalized dispute settlement or conflict resolution, is unduly restrictive if one is interested in getting a picture of the full range of sociolegal occurrences or in grasping differential knowledge of the law. The incidence of full-fledged conflicts of a conceptual or moral order may be high in some areas, such as the regulation of sex and marriage, and extremely low in others, such as property disputes; and the overemphasis on conflict leads to an uneven coverage of the total field of law, especially substantive law. For these critics, the "troublefree" cases of the working systems of property or marriage, for example, become a necessary check on the trouble-case rather than the other way around. There may be an unstated assumption in the anthropology-of-law literature that law knowledge is uniformly distributed and free-flowing, but lawyers know it is not so (Dwyer 1979: 313).

But for Llewellyn, instances of voluntary observance of law constitute invaluable units of analysis because these cases are more apt to round out the feel for and the feel of the law picture (Llewellyn and Hoebel 1941: 40). As a methodological instrument, the trouble-case has limitations for the study of substantive law and its practice, and in fields of law where litigation is rare, researchers may get a skewed idea of law if they focus on the trouble-case. In such circumstances, the study of troublefree practice rather than trouble-cases may indeed be, as Llewellyn and Hoebel wrote, "the safest main road into the discovery of law" (1941: 29).

Nevertheless, *The Cheyenne Way* challenged accepted social science theory. For example, it refuted Durkheim's theory that law moves from punitive sanctions to restitutive sanctions as modern social structures evolve from primitive structures. Although according to Durkheim's evolutionary scheme the Cheyenne were classified among the "primitive" peoples of the world, their law-ways were actually "developed" because restitutive sanctions predominated over punitive ones. Furthermore, Llewellyn and Hoebel also broke new paths with the notions of "drift" and "drive" as they operate in the dynamics of law. Llewellyn and Hoebel brought us to focus on relatively unnoticed changes that have a cumulative impact, as distinct from more recognized, conscious drives for change.

The legal and political context in which Llewellyn and Hoebel wrote gives their work special significance beyond its contribution to social science. The theory of law that Llewellyn was developing was a blow to law school education as it had been practiced before and since Langdell. Llewellyn's theory was also a critique of American judges and the inability of our system to bend with the dynamics of a changing world. The laws of other peoples have often been studied with the expectation that such study would either sustain or challenge current views of law at home. In the seventeenth century, an emphasis on natural law inspired interest in foreign law to prove the universality of natural law principles of the home system. In the eighteenth and nineteenth centuries, many thought that the essence of law was to be found in rules and believed that legislation was a creative force to be used in the molding of society.

In Llewellyn and Hoebel's time, the case system was at the center of legal debate. Cheyenne cases illustrated the idea that the meaning of law was to be found in the wider cultural processes; cases were not isolated instances independent of society. Llewellyn and Hoebel's view of the legal process led them to argue that, even in our own culture, we should include under the rubric of law much more than what is decided by judges in the courts. To see the Cheyenne, then, is to see a good deal of Anglo-American law. The wonderful proficiency that the Cheyenne displayed in handling friction can be instructive in an evaluation of the American system of law and its practitioners. Llewellyn and Hoebel made an important and original contribution by combining, in one volume, the study of "modern" and "primitive" law in such a way that the work of the Cheyenne judges demystified the model of Anglo-American legal reasoning. The ethnographic data provided examples of how law as process operated in synchronism with conventional wisdom. If the Cheyenne were capable of "juristic beauty," then conventional Anglo-American jurisprudes should be capable of humility in the task of reconsidering juridical purpose. Understanding that some cases restored harmony not through the exercise of authority but by means of compromise challenged the notion that order is achieved solely by courts, constables, police, and the law writ through adversarial and punitive procedures.

One reviewer put it more specifically:

> The abundance and intricacy of current material has made us sharp on the doctrine, the rule, the mooted point. But the larger issues of office and outline we are prone to neglect. Intent upon them and for want of a better laboratory the authors are driven back to the usages of a more direct people.. . .It has taken a brilliant use of a superb technique for the authors to say that the life of the law is not observance but function. . .a sermon to the brethren of the American bar. (Hamilton 1943: 233–34)

In sum, then, the jurist and the anthropologist found what they were seeking. A vital part of the juristic-anthropological method is using a wide-angle lens to examine the courts, the judges, and the rules of law themselves. The salient task is to determine how well the law fits the society it purports to serve and how able the law is to meet new contingencies in that society. In the best-case scenario, the institutionalized form limits arbitrariness and passion. Though criticism of legal dogmas of the past may result in a *theory* of law as the expression of the social opinion of the generation whose law it is, realistic jurisprudence offers a way of fusing the notion of *practice* with the notion of "standard," by arguing the superiority of method over content. But anthropologists or outsiders to the jurisprudential debates do not readily grasp the broader intellectual significance of *The Cheyenne Way*—that is, they do not recognize it as a critique of law school education and as a criticism of American judges and the seeming inability of our system to meet the challenge of rapidly changing circumstances.

The shift of scholarly attention from an emphasis on systems of social control to systems of disputing, from positive inducement to the handling of norm violation after the fact, was a predictable result of the narrowing of the subject matter and collegial interaction between anthropologists and American-trained lawyers. Whereas Malinowski (1926) had deliberately formulated a wide-angle framework for understanding law in society, Llewellyn and Hoebel restricted the focus to public forums. Using a technique adumbrated by others, Llewellyn and Hoebel's work on the Cheyenne marked the beginning of many years of concentration on the "trouble-case" approach, with social scientists examining how law breaking is handled in a society. Thenceforth, the unit of analysis was the case, and more often than not, the case as handled through public means. Not surprisingly, this kind of specialization resulted in theories that were more static, more correlational, less concerned with change, even though anthropologists were often studying societies in states of rapid change brought on by political, religious, and economic colonialism.

THE PERIOD OF
EURO-AMERICAN HEGEMONY

From the late 1960s to the mid-1990s, lawyers and anthropologists intersected frequently as the sheer numbers of both increased. Some lawyers became anthropologists. Some anthropologists became lawyers. But more often than ever before, academic lawyers moved away from technical law toward the impact of the law on everyday life, and in so doing practiced a kind of social science. Others never integrated but instead expanded their domain of interest, literally providing results for the other disciplines through a manner of independent invention, rediscovering, for example, what anthropologists already knew (Zorn 1990). We bumped into one another in the field— in Africa, in New Guinea, in Latin America, on international development projects. We met at law reform conferences in the United States, and we founded scholarly movements such as the Law and Society movement. Critical Legal Studies (CLS) followed with more *picante,* that is, more bite. In short, political and scholarly boundaries became blurred, and so did interests. The politics of law was now a serious intellectual endeavor.

For Llewellyn and Hoebel, far from the political hellholes of their country, the way of the Cheyenne was a catalyst for rethinking the meaning of the interconnections between law and culture. In recapitulating the 1920s and 1930s, contemporary academic intellectuals may have a sense of being there, for the present is also a period of reassessment of dominant ideas across national and disciplinary boundaries and a time to rethink, among other things, the place of law. In the 1990s, law was a matter of global proportion in both its constructed and indigenous forms. After supplanting France and Germany during the 1950s as the leading legal system within the Western legal tradition, American legal culture has now achieved worldwide leadership status (Dezalay and Garth 1996; Mattei 1997: 226–27, 233).

Today there is a new generation of legal realists. CLS is an intellectual movement whose intent is to examine the ideology and practice of Anglo-American law. Once again CLS scholars have adopted cultural analysis as a method; although they seldom partner with anthropologists, and they have no intent to study the exotic other. Instead, they are exoticizing the contemporary American scene. Using ethnographic and literary techniques, they examine legal education, discourse, and tradition and the social effects of law. Their purpose goes beyond realistically describing a working system. Many aspire to understand law as cultural hegemony (Kairys 1982). Ipso facto, documenting hegemony means that they no longer perceive cultures as closed and bounded. There are no harmonious Cheyenne as an escape. Nor are they rethinking interconnections. Their work is paradigm busting. Social theory has replaced social science. David Kairys is clear about why: "As law and justice are increasingly distinct and in conflict," there is "more questioning and interest regarding the social role and functioning of the law than in any other period over the last fifty years" (1982: xi). The concern was to identify law's core, its autonomy; the focus of critical thought was legal ideology. Critical race theory and feminist legal theory were among the results of the CLS movement, which was largely confined to law schools and the law case.

The critical thought of the CLS movement repudiates the idealized model of law operating with a routinized decision-making process and continues in the venue of the legal realism school. According to CLS scholars, the idealized model is false, nonexistent: "The problem is not that courts deviate from legal reasoning. There is no legal reasoning in the sense of a legal

methodology or process for reaching particular, correct results";
for the CLS group, democratizing the law means increasing
"popular participation in the decisions that shape our society
and affect our lives" (Kairys 1982: 3). In so arguing, these scholars expose the fact that under the present system, "powerful,
largely corporate, interests, the patriarchal, authoritarian family,
and, in selected areas, government officials are not to be inter-
fered with, by the courts or by the people." "Traditional jurisprudence," they argue, "ignores social and historical reality with
myths about objectivity and neutrality" (4). They reject notions
of technical expertise and objectivity that serve as vehicles for
maintaining existing power relations. Thus, CLS scholars are
mainly lawyers, are mainly based in the United States, and
mainly write about their own law.

The Law and Society movement gathers in scholars from
law, the fields of social science—sociology, anthropology, psychology, criminology, political science, history—and the hu-
manities, scholars who locate their work both nationally and
internationally. For them, law is not autonomous but embedded
in society and explained by forces outside the law. Originally,
the law and society scholars took their impetus from the United
States' development and modernization activities, dubbed by
one author as "legal imperialism" (Gardner 1980). The Law
and Society movement was initially reformist in nature. Its proponents believed that law could be used to achieve social change
and to remedy inequality and injustice. They ascribed to Western law the intention of promoting freedom and democracy, of
enhancing social equalities in the Third World. Some lawyers
in former colonial sites, such as Papua New Guinea or in Africa,
began to map the separate domains of customary and Western

law in preparation for the creation of new nation-state law. However, when these development lawyers came home, their experience abroad translated for some into law and society work at home (Friedman 1986). There were, of course, exceptions, such as Richard Abel of UCLA Law School, who in addition to his legal training earned a degree in anthropology and pursued a myriad interests in Africa and as well as in the United States.

Some scholars came out of the law and modernization efforts with cross-disciplinary training and for a time effected change in law school curricula. For example, in 1971, David Trubek organized the Law and Modernization Program, in which I was a half-year teaching partner, at the Yale Law School. Trubek, who was very much a part of the law and modernization project in Brazil that James Gardner (1980) chronicles, and I taught a core course heavily oriented toward Weberian social science and ethnographic theory and methodology, and many interesting students participated in the course. The Yale Law School program financed, for example, the fieldwork in Rio de Janeiro of Boaventura de Sousa Santos, who was trained in law and philosophy. Using ethnographic techniques, he studied a squatter settlement, a favela he calls "Pasagarda." Later on in his career, he was involved in the CLS movement and in the exploration of the notion of "informal justice." In his book *Toward a New Common Sense: Law, Science, and Politics in a Paradigmatic Transition* (1995), Santos localizes power in the state, in law, and in science. He speaks of the "plurality of legal orders" in the context of globalization. The book is his contribution toward a paradigmatic theory of legal change.

From a more grounded, nonacademic perspective, neither

Critical Legal Studies nor Law and Society is as immediately involved in activism as Lewis Henry Morgan, the movement efforts of Karl Llewellyn, the law and economics neoliberal activists, or the public interest law activists. Indeed, it is only the exceptional instance, such as those community groups found in Madison, Wisconsin, in which academic contributors interact with other law movements, such as the public interest law movement. Public interest work does not generally attract much attention from anthropologists or law school professors in terms of either activism or published work. Disdain of such work is justified by some because of the reformist rather than revolutionary goals of public interest people, by others because they think public interest work is revolutionary rather than reformist. Interestingly, the only major figure of our times who called his own law project revolutionary was President Reagan. However, he did not admit to the economic implications of his law project.

The Law in Economics movement is most commonly associated with the Chicago School of economics and Judge Richard Posner. This movement is one of two examples in which a social science paradigm, namely, economics, replaced legal jurisprudence in United States antitrust law. (The other example, from psychology, I mention later in relation to Alternative Dispute Resolution.) Ellen Hertz's analysis of this paradigm shift is counterintuitive:

> Why have lawyers, usually amply able to protect themselves, allowed the legal subdiscipline of antitrust jurisprudence to be taken over by an economic paradigm? Indeed, this phenomenon is not limited to antitrust law: it has repercussions in tort law, contract, property, and environ-

mental law as well. The answer, I believe, lies in *the declin-ing faith among legal scholars that law is or should be an autonomous discipline* [my emphasis]. This critique of law comes from many directions—critical legal studies, femi-nism, law and economics, law and literature—and it is generally a move one might applaud. However, in this in-stance. . .one of its effects has been to weaken the law's ability to take a position on the morality of business.
(1991: 2)

According to Hertz, who is herself both a lawyer and an an-thropologist, this phenomenon is not law *and* economics, nor is it law *and* anthropology. It is about the shifting dynamics of hegemonic paradigms—Chicago School economics and the Harvard School antitrust paradigm, and the readiness with which President Ronald Reagan replaced heads of the Depart-ment of Justice's antitrust division, the Federal Trade Com-mission, and many federal judgeships with Chicago economists, thereby turning around antitrust enforcement 180 degrees.

Old-style neoclassical economics at the University of Chicago began in the 1930s and 1940s with people like Frank Knight and Henry Simon and then moved into the new Chicago School of the 1950s, 1960s, and 1970s (led notably by Aaron Director, with students such as Posner and Robert Bork). This history of the two periods is crucial because it shows how the new Chicago School economics have altered, even perverted, the original ide-als of neoclassical economics by taking its theoretical assump-tions—that market information is equally available to all; that corporations will constantly strive for higher profits, lower costs, and more efficient production; that entry into industry is costless—as accurate representations of the real world, in spite of numerous and famous critiques of these assumptions by economists such as Joan Robinson. What was initially viewed as a "radical fringe" (Posner's term) came to be taken seriously and—buttressed by the assertion that antitrust law was stifling American business in a strongly competitive international environment—eventually replaced the Harvard School antitrust paradigm. This book is not the place to elaborate this story, but anthropologists might be intrigued to explore what makes certain paradigms succeed in the absence of "fact or evidence" and how such paradigms change the rules of the legal game.[2]

Public interest law is the name given to work done in the public (not private) interest by lawyers mostly outside the academic world. and often associated with the work of Ralph Nader. American public interest lawyers work on structural issues, such as health and safety, that involve not only the courts but also other branches of government. Their interest is often preventative. Discussions of their efforts have appeared in a plethora of books written for the public (e.g., R. Nader 1965; Wasserstein and Green 1970; Green 1975; R. Nader and Smith 1996), and often their efforts are documented in the *Congressional Record,* in current journals, and in the national and in-

2. The anthropological reader might gain some courage in such an endeavor by reading Richard A. Posner's "A Theory of Primitive Society, with Special Reference to Law" (1980). Although it is an example of primitive thinking, a combination of hubris, half-truths, essentialisms, and distortions, the article is nevertheless stimulating, much in the way science fiction is. Posner has anthropomorphized the market and reduced "primitive society" to a recipe in order to prove that the legal and other social institutions of primitive society are economically rational because they value efficiency.

ternational press. Unlike the academics who write about daily
life but are removed from it, public interest lawyers are actively
lobbying for change. And sometimes their opponents are part
of yet another law movement—law and economics—which
has also only peripherally involved anthropologists.

Public interest lawyers work for a just society as defined by
the high expectation levels of those who founded this great
political democracy. They are motivated by the fact that the
number of claims filed in the United States today (nine out of
ten wrongfully injured people do not file a claim) is low compared with the number of civil suits per capita filed in the early
nineteenth century. They are concerned with economic barriers
to justice and with the attempt to preempt the common law of
torts. Because the consumer is a focal concern, public interest
lawyers treat standard contracts of adhesion and the attendant
giving up of rights to go to court as perversions of justice. The
public interest professionals see lawyers as the architects of justice in our society, as people with a mission to address the mal-
distribution of power and its relation to justice issues.

Of these four movements, the Law and Society movement
is the site of most of the overlap between anthropologist and
lawyer academics, mainly in the context of the Law and Society
Association; and as I noted, with the exception of minor forays,
such as testifying in Indian land claims, facilitating mediation,
or laying bare sham mediation procedures, we anthropologists
are not commonly found in direct action research relative to
law in the United States. The anthropologists who are members
of the Law and Society Association overlapped with the lawyers' project. A number of anthropologists began to work in
the United States, which few had done previously, or at least

they worked in the Western world, on issues of increasing interest to law professors. Anthropologists Sally Merry (1990), Barbara Yngvesson (1993a), and Carol Greenhouse, Barbara Yngvesson, and David Engle (1993) worked on issues of class, region, and local communities. Although what they wrote can be read in the tradition of cultural critique, some anthropology of law as practiced in the Law and Society Association lost the primacy of a comparative perspective gained from fieldwork in non-Western sites. Other anthropologists went abroad—to Tibet, the Pacific, the Caribbean, Africa, and elsewhere—and they produced the first of a genre of anthropology of law in the context of globalization. For the first time, anthropologists were forced to address the limits of their naïveté, and in this regard the American Bar Foundation in Chicago became a catalyst.[3]

Elsewhere, too, we find new thinking. Most Italian law and society scholars are trained in the law and are less nation-centered than their American counterparts but well-read in the anthropological literature. Some of the Italian work carried on in the Horn of Africa is interdisciplinary: it includes not just lawyers but also historians, political scientists, sociologists, and anthropologists. They seek to reveal the dynamic and unstable relationships between transplanted "modern" and "traditional" legal systems (Grande 1995). The role of law is, of course, a key to understanding the dynamics of power not only in the Horn but also, for instance, in the European community. The ethnography of law requires an understanding of those who seek to construct larger legal orders with fixed and uniform legali-

3. See, for example, Lazarus-Black and Hirsch, *Contested States: Law, Hegemony, and Resistance* (1994).

ties. Such work includes as objects of study the modernizers, the colonizers, the neocolonized, and those who still heavily depend on customary proceedings even as found in international conferences. The contemporary "civilizing mission" of law by Africans, by Europeans, and by Americans is more than a story of crises in legal pluralism. It is a story about cultural transformation, sometimes discovered through the analysis of legal documents (Riles 2000).

Nevertheless, what is at times referred to as an "epistemological crisis" in the academic studies of law directs attention to dichotomous discourses. Law is many things—it is a *reflection* of society eternally new; it is *molded by* economics and society; it is an *instrument* used by people in power, people whose hands are on the controls; it is a *rational* actor's model associated with empirical research, functionalism, and defense of the status quo. Those who oppose such views stress the role of ideology, that is, the symbolic as well as instrumental uses of law in which ideas play a major role. Because the arena is here full of contingencies, ambiguities, and uncertainties, the law and its participants are granted a degree of autonomy. From such a viewpoint, law becomes a semi-independent source of authority and not just a reflection of the balance of power, and the anthropologist pushes the analysis of law toward a more interactive and comparative model.

The self-conscious attempts of legal scholars to break with instrumentalism have spawned a whole host of dichotomies: meaning versus behavior, hegemony versus hermeneutics, ideology versus practice, meaning versus material relations, structure versus practice. Yet in the process of trying to save postempirical social science from Machiavellianism, from being "all politics," some have gone beyond mere posturing and have taken a curious position of interpretive analysis without politics.

In sum, there has been a virtual revolution in thinking about law by lawyers and anthropologists in these different contexts. The law and modernization movement (or legal development) sought (and still seeks) to democratize the so-called Third World by exporting European and American legal education and legal codes and statutes, thought to be an inexpensive kind of development that is currently being reapplied in Eastern Europe, India, Africa, and elsewhere. The Law and Society Association made a niche for scholars who in the 1960s and early 1970s were few and marginal in their home schools. The CLS movement led to a progressive examination of the assumptions of American law and legal education, an examination that revealed that the law was more political than neutral. Public interest lawyers were researching the realities of corporate crime and violation of law in the United States—in relation to air, water, land, regulatory agencies, dams, and air and auto safety among other topics—and around the globe as they monitored the behavior of multinational corporations abroad. The Chicago-style Law in Economics movement loosely paralleled the Reagan revolution and what continues to follow from it. There were exciting discoveries, such as the finding that law is still a powerful vehicle for cultural transmissions or legal imperialisms or counterhegemonic forces. However, finding on home ground the same patterns that we encountered abroad brought a crisis of contradictions.

To my mind, many of these intellectual movements may now be approaching dead ends, sometimes because, as in the law and society work, the research is more and more replicating the very thing many sought to escape — boundary controls. The CLS movement has its own problems, often caught in disembodied literatures and narrative techniques that center on discourse-based positions to the exclusion of other factors found in action. Nevertheless, my many conversations with law school colleagues have made it clear that mainstream legal thought that was absorbed with narrow technical views has been severely shaken, both conceptually and methodologically. And for me, all this activity, both in an out of the academic world, has been stimulating and inspiring. What needs to be done has become clearer.

From the perspective of anthropology, which may have given more than it received during the past thirty years of intellectual gymnastics, we have profited. Anthropologists learned about the power of law and the power *in* law, something that is obvious to lawyers. The view from below has expanded upward and outward. Anthropologists consistently underestimated (and still do) the role of legal ideologies in the construction or deconstruction of culture writ large. However, we now include legal transplants, missionary justice, USAID or foreign aid programs, UN-sponsored international conferences with their legal documents, and economic globalization as part of the local ethnographic picture. In other words, the broadened intellectual context that anthropologists are working in today is at least part of our active thought, whether in understanding the impact of colonialism, or the Cold War, or the competition for world resources. Earlier anthropological notions of cultural critique and comparison, of culture and local knowledge, and the various ideas about pluralism have moved horizontally into sister disciplines. Anthropologists are in a strong position to reap theoretical harvest from this ferment and to explore new ethnographic ground.

For example, anthropologists and legal scholars are currently generating a most interesting body of work by combining history and ethnography. They now ask questions that were avoided during earlier periods: How has law served the "civilizing mission" of colonialism, and how by such means are societies of the Third World and the law of the West being transformed? How has cultural reformation became part of the strategies of local elites? In other words, how have small-scale legal events, shaped by large-scale transformations, become instruments of the global social system? If this historical work is depoliticized by means of structural arrangement discourse, it is also clearly encompassing power models. That is, both the blindness and the transformative aspects of colonialism are there in the literature along with contemporary contestations. The view that is still with us today, of colonized peoples as primitive and disordered and in need of being transformed by plans that are fixed, abstracted, and disembodied, is part of the culture of expanding capitalist economies with which such transformation is more compatible. Changing intellectual styles that are more inclusive and less restrictive raise questions about notions of customary or modern law and imposed and indigenous law as diverse systems of law work for various interest groups.

Over the past twenty years, historical and comparative research into law and colonialism has had a major intellectual impact, its central achievement being the enlarged and innovative perspective of law professors who overlap with anthropologists in "the field." There are dangers as well as benefits here, a point well elaborated by James Gardner (1980) in his book *Legal Imperialism: American Lawyers and Foreign Aid in Latin America,* in which he analyzes the consequences of the exportation of a legal model that is flawed both for Latin America and for the United States. Perhaps the best autobiographical statement of professional invigoration is that of Marc Galanter (1989); in his *Law and Society in Modern India,* he revisits the manner in which his experience in India forced him to rethink American law problems. The unlearning of fundamental assumptions and conceptual frameworks has not fully worked itself out; but in American law schools the contradictions are clearer, and the fight is on as the field of inquiry continues to expand rather than contract. The language in which law is being cast is increasingly part of society-wide debates, which, as earlier comments indicate, are double-edged, as in the intersections between anthropologists, lawyers, Aboriginal women, and participants at human rights conventions, for example.[4]

And so, as we begin the twenty-first century, both lawyers and anthropologists are once again, as were their nineteenth-century forebears, concerned with global scale, with history, with power, with democracies and plutocracies, with contested domains, and with evangelical missions. The bottom may have fallen out of history in the nineteenth century, but twentieth-century legal scholars were still debating clashing notions of the

4. Diane Bell, an anthropologist who has long studied gender, law, and power among Australian Aborigines, asks, "How is it that lawyers have become the new paternalists? Why is it that the limits of the rights to be enjoyed by any one group is what white male lawyers find reasonable?" (1992: 356).

role of law in the nature of change; and the bottom may be falling out of law as we enter the twenty-first century. Indeed, one of Italy's distinguished comparative law experts, Professor Rodolfo Sacco (1996), is entirely correct in urging a macrohistoric perspective, one that goes far beyond the recent past as found in legal history written as usual. Professor Sacco reminds us, as does the anthropological literature on law, of other legal traditions past and present, traditions in which the function— that is, the use—of law was precedent to any individual design. Law can exist and evolve without lawyers as sovereign power, or even without the state. The state has not always existed, and various systems of law can and do coexist or compete. Contemplation of the life of the law in our contemporary world perforce returns us to an earlier time when power was conferred in the exclusive economic interest of those who held it. Should not a legal "history" turn to the future to question what may from the past not appear self-evident today? It may be obvious to conclude that the way law is constituted and the way it is portrayed work side by side with the law in action, but, if not, I hope this observation will become clearer in the pages that follow.

THREE

Hegemonic Processes in Law
Colonial to Contemporary

The popular element "feels" but does not always know or
understand; the intellectual element "knows" but does
not always understand and in particular does not always feel.
Antonio Gramsci

Placing the law firmly within the more general categories of
social and cultural control, or controlling processes more specifically, has been one of the most important results of enlarging
the stage and multiplying the tools for discovery. Recognizing
the multiple jurisdictions of law—"indigenous," colonial, religious, or nation-state law—underscores the idea that law is
often not a neutral regulator of power but instead the vehicle
by which different parties attempt to gain and maintain control
and legitimization of a given social unit. Nor is law that which
stands between us and anarchy, for the lack of state-centered
legal systems has not been found to be associated with anarchy.
On the contrary, in stateless societies, law is associated with
powerful plaintiffs rather than with powerful lawyers. And
needless to say, the study of law cannot be divorced from ideologies that make control of law a prize.

A colleague who is both anthropologist and lawyer once urged:

> It thus remains for us. . .to confront the two realms—ideology and order-maintenance—in tandem, and to ascertain their role in the processual sphere by extending the anthropology of law's strong focus on dispute processing. . . .Gramsci's emphasis on the difference between the state and civil society, and his perception of how the two interweave, are useful as an integrative first framework for this sort of analysis. (Dwyer 1979: 316)

Ideas about culture are interwoven with notions of control and the dynamics of power. Anthropologists of law know that dispute resolution ideologies have long been used for the transmission of hegemonic ideas, but this knowledge has yet to be extended beyond those who study disputing processes. Thus, the study of structures and activities that cross boundaries can illuminate places where power is being reconfigured and reconstituted, but one must first recognize power as something to be reckoned with in building theories of everyday life activities.

In this third chapter, continuing a subject touched on earlier, I examine hegemonic processes as they work in or on law from colonial to contemporary settings and across changing structures. World conditions have stimulated anthropologists to work at the junctures of the local and the global in order to locate populations in larger currents. The local by itself does not contain explanatory possibilities. Eric Wolf's book *Europe and the People without History* (1982) shaped my understanding of the need to erase the boundaries between Western and non-Western history, to make connections that had for so long been absent from earlier efforts to document and explain the spread of dominant legal models. The research strategies needed to make these connections involve combinations of ethnographic, historical, and critical approaches. Ethnography gets to the core of control, history connects us to process, and reflexivity requires us to examine assumptions and normalized behaviors and to document how dominant ideas in law are manufactured and how and why they travel. For instance, theories of social evolution alert us to the role of the state in the evolving roles of plaintiffs and defendants as they increase or decrease their power to litigate.

Studying social transformation by means of hegemonies necessitates looking at the numerous ways in which law at first glance appears acceptable or neutral. Antonio Gramsci's notion of hegemony is about the assumptions of existing order that are accepted by dominated and dominant alike, about the clusters of belief that circumscribe that which is considered natural, the way things are and should be. Hegemony is about obtaining consent and legitimacy, about dominance and subordination, both constraining and enabling. Thus, both the vertical and the horizontal axes are relevant to any observation of the makeup and workings of hegemonic power, especially in the configuring or reconfiguring culture by means of language. My research on controlling processes is also about clusters of beliefs that may narrow options and foreclose different ideas and futures. Not all of these controlling processes start out as hegemonic or even counterhegemonic (Nader 1997).[1] For instance, explaining the

1. Antonio Gramsci referred to hegemony in two forms: hegemony as organized by intellectuals, the "dominant group's 'disputes'" (Gramsci

privatization of justice would require recognition of a cluster of beliefs that since the beginning of the twentieth century have triggered a transition from an ethic of right and wrong to an ethic of treatment. In the right ideological climate, the ethic of right and wrong recedes, and disputes are not resolved through its application but rather disappear through an ethic of treatment related to psychotherapy (Claeson 1994). But I am getting ahead of my story.

What I wish to elaborate on here is the contemporary spread of a specific cluster of beliefs that I refer to as harmony ideology and that operate as control by limiting the playing field to a recurrent dialectic between legality and its alternatives. The story is a long history of continuity, in which colonial dichotomies used to control the "uncivilized" are transferred to contemporary legal arenas along with the same ideologies of control. It appears to be exactly by means of binary thinking, as in the move from the adversarial law model to the harmony model, that legal remedies are controlled at the local and international levels. As I intimated earlier, in this kind of research, we must carry out the internal and external analyses at the same

---

1971: 12), and the "conquest of hegemony by a subaltern class," what some call "counterhegemony." See also Sassoon, *Gramsci's Politics* (1987). Although hegemony may imply the control of the masses by dominant classes, the nature of the acquiescence—that is, the effectiveness of hegemonic structures of thought—is open to interpretation. Hegemonic ideas can be considered to be in flux, constructed and reconstructed by various actors and institutions operating in diverse contexts. Comaroff and Comaroff's (1921: 3) view that hegemony should be distinguished from culture and ideology contrasts with Gramsci's view, with which I concur, of hegemony as "ideology in its highest sense."

time in order to know how sets of cultural meanings came about. Thus, instead of speaking of autonomous or semiautonomous fields, we acknowledge that law is transformed by seemingly external forces. The fields are not stationary, and exact points of origin and exact boundaries become illusory the more we come to know of the social spaces in which law is produced. It is precisely because law is so closely tied to, rather than reflective of, implicit social assumptions that we need to consider its social and cultural organization.

THE HARMONY LEGAL MODEL
AND LEGAL CENTRALISM

I recently attended a conference that dealt with the need for peacemaking and conflict-management practices in Africa. The cast of characters reflected both colonial and contemporary interests in that continent. There were Africans from all over the continent, social scientists, peace specialists, military personnel, and other interested parties. The meeting was opened by the distinguished son of an African chief. The terms he used— peace and harmony—and his references to the negativity of the Muslims to the north might have been uttered by missionaries only a few decades ago, or even today. Idealist Africans were also there, extolling the virtues of precolonial conflict resolution medicine, as if reinventing tradition could solve problems in dealing with mercenaries. Western negotiation theorists commented on the "software" (their term for negotiation techniques). Nationalists argued for structures that mirrored the needs of indigenous populations. American peacekeeping strategists discussed the possibility of including indigenous "customary" strategies in conflict management. Nobody suggested that foreign involvement in local communities might be generating or exacerbating conflict, and peacekeeping professionals portrayed African peoples as bellicose rather than stable. Missing from most of the presentations were the political economy of conflict management and the particular history of the African continent. There was no talk of arms dealing, of diasporas that organized some of the traffic in arms, no talk of multinationals, of natural resources, of international agencies, or of the World Court. Nobody held the view that peace and harmony might be an ideology of oppression. Most participants presented ongoing internal analyses about managing regional and ethnic conflict by means of what I recognized as an ideology of harmony—a form of pacification by means, on the surface at least, antagonistic to legal centralism.[2] For the outside observer, harmony ideology appeared to be a policy position considered "natural" and quite compatible with the needs of the multinational organizations of global economies. Whether this ideology was compatible with the values of human freedom and justice was not discussed. The participants were not thinking "outside the box," a phrase that suggests that at least some recognize closed cognitive models.

Not long after the conference, I noticed that the U.S. Naval War College was developing a variety of strategies to move

2. See Franz von Benda-Beckmann, "Citizens, Strangers, and Indigenous Peoples" (1997) for clarification on the manner in which ideological commitment determines the conceptualizations of legal pluralism as either fully embraced or vehemently rejected by etatist conservative thinkers and by liberals and leftists alike.

"obstructionist leaders" toward cooperation. Obstructionist leaders are warlords or strongmen: "high-level indigenous leaders in civil conflicts who are bent on obstructing international efforts to deliver humanitarian aid and advance peace" ("Dealing" 1998: 5). Of course, someone has to decide who is obstructionist. These examples are pieces of harmony ideology in which coercion, and pacification goals, are barely concealed.

I mentioned earlier that as a result of my Zapotec work (Nader 1990) I outlined a theory of harmony ideology as pacification, as a tool used by the Spanish Crown through the missionaries, first in the colonization of Mexico and then in other colonies in the New World. By means of "missionary courts," missionaries set up what we increasingly recognize from other sites as encapsulated models of harmony. The military and the political government followed the missionaries, but only after the Spanish Crown had legally placed the indigenous peoples in "autonomous" village units, a free space that eventually enabled the Zapotec to use harmony as a counterhegemonic tool *against* superordinate power holders.

My colleague Elizabeth Colson, who has worked among Native Americans as well as Africans, draws an interesting contrast between the British rule of African indigenous communities and the United States' rule of Native Americans (Colson 1974). The British had a policy of indirect rule that made it possible for Africans to resist superordinate power under the guise of tradition. However, Native Americans were denied local autonomy because the United States was pursuing a policy of cultural assimilation, and Indian institutions were seen as a barrier to assimilation. The story of how native peoples' nations were reduced in their rights to self-government is a story of incremental control, step by step, act by act, all heading toward termination and relocation until the Indian Civil Rights Act of 1968.

The American Indian movement of the 1960s was fueled by the outrage against federal initiatives, not the least of which brought corporations onto Indian lands. From that point (and maybe earlier), the people of the reservations were split into the traditionalists and the accommodationists. A search for tradition through mediation (or identity politics) accompanied Indian activism. The rise of mediation among American Indians paralleled the Alternative Dispute Resolution (ADR) movement in mainstream American society. The representation of Indian justice as informal and consensual rather than adjudicative was a representation promoted by the white judiciary as well as by Native Americans. Both parties agreed to believe that peacekeeping was an old and time-honored tradition among Native Americans. At the same time, native peoples' litigation proceeded, owing to national legal assistance: the very fact that litigation was an option encouraged negotiation, since litigation becomes an option when negotiation fails. Relevant to the issue of using harmony as a hegemonic tool is the study of the differential use of idealizations in the struggle over nuclear waste storage on Indian land (Nader and Ou 1998). The struggle between proponents and opponents of storage on reservations rapidly intensified, with all sides in the negotiation— the Indians, the United States government, and the nuclear waste industry—claiming the true Indian way.

Once it was clear that Indian tribes were the most politically feasible hosts for nuclear waste, the U.S. Office of the Nuclear Waste Negotiator, in concert with key proponents of tribal economic development, went all-out in identifying and utilizing cultural variables with which to market the storage of nuclear wastes.[3] As noted in Bill Maurer's British Virgin Islands ethnography, tribal sovereignty was a mirage because, for reasons of security and safety, any Indian monitored retrievable storage (MRS) host would have to be placed under great scrutiny and control by federal agencies.[4] Waiving the right to sue in a case where a reservation became a de facto permanent nuclear waste site would in fact be a blow to tribal sovereignty. The very distinction between internal and external is put into question as cultural concepts as well as economic and political models are borrowed, shared, and appropriated across the spectrum of power in Indian country. A hierarchy of values is hidden in legal notions of idealizations, particularly in ones that value harmony over conflict or confrontation or adversarial activities. Yet examples abound, as indicated by the American Revolution, that disputing may be a means to harmony and to autonomy and self-determination; and conflict may be part of the struggle in life that keeps people bound together.

Far from being novel, similar transformative techniques of

3. A 1987 amendment to the 1982 Nuclear Waste Policy Act established the Office of the Nuclear Waste Negotiator. The negotiator had the express goal of finding a voluntary host among states and Indian tribes for temporary monitored retrievable storage (MRS) and permanent high-level nuclear waste storage.

4. For an analysis of the social and environmental impact of nuclearism (the driving ideology of the nuclear power industry) on Native Americans from the 1940s through the Cold War and into the 1990s, see Valerie L. Kuletz, *The Tainted Desert: Environmental and Social Ruin in the American West* (1998).

pacification, which later became counterhegemonic tools in many places, now seem likely to have been used throughout Africa by European colonial powers. A legal ideology characterized by the idea that agreement and conciliation are ipso facto better than conflict models minimized disruptions to the civilizing processes. When legal historian Martin Chanock (1985) synthesized documentary materials from two former British colonies, he revealed the early connections between local law and Christian missions, which from the early 1800s were much involved in dispute settlements that used a blend of a Victorian interpretation of biblical law and English procedures known to them. According to Chanock, the missionaries were glad to be peacemakers and to hand down Christian judgment. Doing so was part of the civilizing mission, and as Sally Merry (2000) has persuasively argued, it was so elsewhere and still is. And as I mentioned previously, in the past (and the present), with increased colonization, the pronouncements of "missionary courts" commonly evolved into local "customary" law, which still emphasized conciliation and compromise in accordance with European Christian harmony ideology. Anthropologists later mistook these values for remnants of indigenous customary law, not seeing that compromise in colonial African "customary law" may have become the politics of adjustment for survival purposes.

A similar story unravels in the Pacific. Missionaries first arrived in the 1820s, and they are still coming. Unlike the African analyses, with their historical perspective, contemporary ethnographic studies in New Guinea are documenting the work of missionaries as it is occurring today. These studies of how the introduction of Christian morality operates as mind colonization allow us to ruminate on the central role of the disputing processes in the transformation of native culture and organization to fit the demands of the modern nation-state. Fine-grained fieldwork indicates how coercive harmony operates to silence disputing indigenous peoples who speak or act angrily. Anthropologist Marie Reay documents her observation in New Guinea that the "missions had been playing a part in pacifying the warlike clans and prohibiting violence in interpersonal relations" (1974: 219–20). In a more recent ethnography on the subject of colonizing legal transformations, Merry (2000: 63) tells the story of New England missionaries and lawyers and the process of legal transformation: "The adoption of Anglo-American law was inextricably joined into the adoption of Christianity, a severe Calvinist version of Protestant Christianity brought by stern, impassioned, and ethnocentric missionaries from New England." Interestingly, in the 1980s, when I was developing my ideas on the connection between law and missionizing, there were scarcely any ethnographic materials linking the two—such are the blind spots that we must continuously search to reveal.

It is difficult to grasp the process of mind colonization, especially if it happens slowly and incrementally over many years. The New Guinea ethnographies offer a clear idea of the way in which the introduction of Christian morality affects the disputing process. For example, Edward Schieffelin (1981), who analyzed evangelical rhetoric as it relates to the transformation of traditional culture in Papua New Guinea, was able to penetrate the drama as it relates to disputing processes. He emphasized the function of rhetoric as "the vehicle by which the message is rendered into a social construction upon reality."

Traditionally, the regulation of conduct between individuals was a matter to be settled by those involved, and such regulation was guided by the canons of reciprocity and sanctioned by the threat of retaliation or revenge. Christianity regards one's conduct toward others as a matter not between two persons but between each individual and God: "The fundamental direction of moral reciprocity was moved from the horizontal plane between people to the vertical between man and God mediated by pastor and church organization" (155). Amity was the goal of the Christian efforts at dispute management, a goal predicated on the belief that the ideal state of human society is "harmony."

Before colonial pacification, quarreling was tolerated and even enjoyed in New Guinea. Epstein (1974) noted that amity is a cultural value to which different societies attach different weight. And who can say in this age of ubiquitous military hardware that amity is not a social value that all societies should share? Such a question is a poignant one for observers of New Guinea and Indonesia, where ethnographers are describing the stratigraphy of legal influences with the added dimensions of the state and multinational mining groups (Hyndman 1994; Gordon and Meggitt 1985). Current work on the interlocking of missionary, state, and corporate economic interests, which are often justified through legal means, indicates fruitful areas for research on the law in economics and religion (Colby with Dennett 1995).

In South Africa, we have almost a reversal of the examples already cited. The basis for contemporary nation-building in South Africa incorporated in the 1996 constitution and the Truth and Reconciliation Commission (TRC) requires loyalty to a national and international world rather than to local tribal and community affiliations. Thus the struggle over whether individuals should think about justice in terms of local law or in the language of international and national human rights is a real one. Richard Wilson (2000) argues in "Reconciliation and Revenge in Post-Apartheid South Africa" that no matter how powerful apologies of reconciliation may be in the emergent South Africa, people in the townships diverge from greater state centralization because they look for justice in punishment and revenge, not in reconciliation. Wilson's description of the processes of the TRC, a commission founded on the notions of transnational human rights and Christian ethics of forgiveness and redemption, is disturbing. The new South Africa is using truth and reconciliation to lay out the larger picture of what happened during apartheid and to prevent the escalation of violence, but what the move from state violence to state harmony will mean is not at all clear, especially when that move is coercive. Law has taken at least three directions one after the other since World War II. The first was the development and spread of a United Nations human rights movement that had its roots in Euro-American liberal philosophy. The second was an attack on the civil litigation and rights consciousness in the United States, an attack that launched the ADR movement. The third direction was the combination of the secular and the sacred, for example, the combination of ADR and Christianity. The morality of disputing processes is now everywhere heavily influenced by religious ideologies that are hidden in national, transnational, and hegemonic discourses.

In *Reconciliation: What Does It Mean?* (1999), Gary Johns and anthropologist Ron Brunton, who is a critic of the aboriginal quest for sovereign rights, discuss reconciliation in Australia. A biting review of this work by Ian McIntosh (2000) examines the promise of reconciliation. Johns and Brunton suggest that reconciliation is about providing Aborigines with a measure of autonomy to help readjustment, allowing economic development on aboriginal lands for the greater common good, and facilitating the movement of Aborigines, since their lifestyle in remote locales is uneconomic and unsustainable. McIntosh draws the line: "The basic premise that Aborigines must change as a precondition of reconciliation is problematic." McIntosh supports a pan-Australian identity model that incorporates Aborigines as equals; contrast his view with that of Brunton and Johns, who say there is no surviving pan-Aboriginal collective with which non-Aborigines can reconcile, only a motley collection of scattered tribes and individuals. Such conceptions are reflected in court outcomes where Aborigines have no standing because critics believe that there is next to nothing left of their laws or that they have none; there is not even enough with which to reconcile!

In the 1980s the study of hegemonic movements was of particular interest to anthropologists who had been enmeshed in what we thought of as more traditional culture, only to find similar patterns closer to home. Carol Greenhouse's book about Georgia Baptists, *Praying for Justice* (1986), illustrates by means of cultural analysis the close ties between religious tenets and disputing processes. Law, indeed, is part of culture, and Georgia Baptists are of special interest to anthropologists who wish to understand the way in which Baptist Protestant fundamentalism fits into political and legal reform movements at the national level. Greenhouse believes that for Georgia Baptists, all conflict is inner conflict: harmony is an inner search, and public remedy gives way to God's remedy. People thus deal with conflict by internalizing it and seeking internal remedies, in the belief that conflict stems from a person's character and from a rejection of God. Baptists refuse to concede the adversarial element; the alternative to disputing is a brotherhood that is antiauthoritarian and egalitarian. Dissent is eliminated by "withdrawal." Baptists equate Christianity with harmony and the rejection of adversarial disputing. Even though the Baptist past is one of conflict, the true Baptist acts of conflict resolution symbolize a kind of cultural cleansing of that past as harmonious and ahistoric. Whereas the Zapotec have a conception of harmony that requires them to litigate to find harmony, among Greenhouse's informants it is the silencing of disputes that needs understanding. Greenhouse presents us with the valorization of powerlessness: only God, not people, can do something about auto accidents, nuclear accidents, poison in our water, and so on.

Harmony ideology is significant in the light of expanding Protestant fundamentalism in the United States and in the light of an ADR law-reform program that may silence disagreement for the sake of achieving consensus and adopting a worldview that transforms facts and legal rights into feelings, relationships, and community writ small. One might argue that since the 1960s, Americans have been "civilized" in a process not so very different from that which Merry (2000) describes for the Hawaiians. By positioning culture in history, Greenhouse and Merry show that cultural rationalities stem from social practices, but they also discover the depth of interconnections between religion, law, and order, interconnections that might be obvious to scholars who are practicing believers rather than secular academics.

Also in North America, Norman Forer (1979), examining the historic roots of the process of legal imposition on American Indians, notices that the United States supported church missionaries in their task of persuading the Indian to accept private rather than collective entrepreneurship and resettlement. In the contemporary era, missionizing in the reservations has never been more active. In India, the state—in the guise of the Company Raj, Imperial India, or modern India—also promoted "arbitration" and "compromise," an ideal most persistently expressed as "Panchayat justice." This history of the rise and spread of the idea of Panchayat justice is still being written, but legal scholars generally concede that its political intent is pacification, a quieting of the population (Meschievitz and Galanter 1982).

When theorists speak of cultural control as hegemony, they are not usually speaking of culture as such, but rather of culture that is constructed in one place and then moves out, much as colonies of people do, to settle in distant lands. An early indication that state and religious laws may create new forms of nonstate law is the example of sixteenth-century Castile, where compromise was the ideal and preferred means for ending disputes, it being accepted opinion that lawsuits were antithetical to Christian belief. Presumably, Spanish missionaries carried this idea to the New World, while ironically in Spain during that same era, there was an increase in adversarial behavior associated with the rise of trade and commerce (Kagan 1981). Thus, peoples colonized by Europeans on all major continents were being socialized toward conformity and adaptation by means of "customary" law, while at home, adversarial court behavior was on the rise.

All the modern nation-states created as the result of European colonization depend on a legal-centralism model. Yet, as we know, state law is commonly challenged by older systems of law, such as "customary," precolonial, or Islamic law in Africa and the Middle East. Though the idea of legal pluralism sometimes incorporates the plural experience, scholars often do not recognize the hegemonies operating within systems, nor does the scholarship on legal pluralism regularly call attention to the observation that state law may actually create new forms of nonstate law, not just revive old ones.

There may be a close relationship between the management of state law and antilaw or nonstate mechanisms of control, as indicated by the essayists in Elisabetta Grande's book titled *Transplants, Innovation, and Legal Tradition in the Horn of Africa* (1995). In the concluding essay of Grande's volume, Rodolfo Sacco notes that in the Horn of Africa there is a border region between state and stateless and that on both sides of this border, contemporary choices lie between recent European models and "traditional" ones. Professor Sacco points out that when it comes to state structures, the primary issues are democracy, popular sovereignty, and federalism. The situation is further complicated by multiethnicity if the model is that of a privileged ethnic group playing a dominant role over others.

In a more recent volume (Favali, Grande, and Guadagni 1998), several authors point to the nonstate origins of legal change policies that came about with the advent of powerful institutions like the World Bank, the International Monetary Fund, and also USAID. The authors' approach is outside the law, both political law and economic law, and challenges the assumption that the transfer of law is equivalent to just any transfer of technology. Instead these legal scholars underscore the need to understand institutions in context.

Africa is not the only continent where directions in law are being hotly contested. In *Beyond Law,* J. T. Guevara-Gil and Joseph Thome begin their paper "Notes on Legal Pluralism" by quoting a question raised in 1984 by the Bolivian workers' union (Confederación Sindical Única de Trabajadores Campesinos de Bolivia, CSUTCB): "Why is it that Roman and Napoleonic Law are thought better adapted to our reality than our own experience and age-long traditions?" They further note: "This poignant question challenges the whole project of constructing Latin American nation-states as mirror-images of idealized European models of how societies should be organized" (1992: 75). To create national, integrated, and homogenous societies out of multiethnic social and cultural landscapes is for Guevara-Gil and Thome "mission impossible." They call attention to a paradigmatic shift "qualitatively different to any previous ethnocidal, assimilationist, or integrationist effort" as simply the right to be different. They portray the centralizing nation-state as having a "civilizing mission" in which law performs a critical role as a coercive discourse imposed upon society.

The shift is from the ideology of legal centralism to the emergence and practice of "alternative laws." Hegemonic alternatives are by definition ideological; however, Guevara-Gil and Thome continue by quoting law professor John Griffiths, who argues, "Legal pluralism is the fact. Legal centralism is a myth, an ideal, a claim, an illusion." (1986: 4–5). They also note the definition of Boaventura de Sousa Santos (1987: 297–98): "Legal pluralism is the key concept in a postmodern view of law. Not the legal pluralism of traditional legal anthropology in which the different legal orders are conceived as separate entities co-existing. . .[but] an intersection of different legal orders." Santos is proposing not to eliminate legal centralism but just to shake it into becoming polycentric, for him a view from the bottom. Almost as an afterthought, he also realizes that legal centralism is being decentered by a suprastate legality based on establishment of world "law" by the dominant multinational corporations and supranational organizations. Although they recognize extra-state powers, Guevara-Gil and Thome conclude with a discussion of a new legal plurality in the context of squatter settlements, nongovernmental organizations, the right to be different, and the economic crisis in most Latin American nation-states, as if all were somehow unrelated to global economics. For Guevara-Gil and Thome, legal pluralism can serve both as an analytical tool and as a political goal of democratization.

Attention to practice as well as theoretical construct has forced me to a different view of the shake-up to which Santos was referring. The United States is the starting point of a process whereby legal ideologies become forces of change that move out to the international arena. Ideological changes are first shaped through discourse, and such changes go far beyond the law to include the links between law, business, psychiatric, and community constituencies, thereby cutting across professional networks. I have given both historical examples, such as the diffusion of harmony law models during the colonial period, and particular examples, such as the Georgia Baptists or

Hawaiians. I have also spoken of a contemporary example that I have been following since the early 1970s—the Pound conference of 1976, at which the chief justice of the United States formally launched the ADR movement that was to revolutionize law in the United States. Since then, as both a participant and an observer, I have tracked the spread and growth of the ADR movement. Because alternatives to courts were not newly invented in the 1960s, it is perhaps useful to begin with some history.

NATION-STATE PACIFICATION: THE UNITED STATES MODEL

European legal scholars, such as Eugen Ehrlich (1936), and American legal historians have long been cognizant of more or less autonomous entities that refused to recognize state monopoly in law. In his book *Justice without Law?* (1983), historian Jerold Auerbach surveys alternatives to courts in the United States. Drawing examples from the seventeenth century onward, he illustrates how dispute settlement preferences in the United States regularly express personal choice, cultural values, and power disparities. Communities based on ethnicity, religion, class, work, or profession indicate the conditions under which alternatives to legal centralism become shifting commitments in the application of power to serve the legal supremacy of the state. Auerbach's objective is to build a model of dispute settlement history that provides clues to the current enthusiasm for nonlegal alternatives. He develops his narrative about a persistent countertradition to legalism by examining three different types of communities: colonial, Christian utopian, and immigrant. The first colonies were self-contained communities in which conflict was either suppressed or dealt with through mediation. There was either enforced harmony or open schism. The utopian communities, numbering well more than a hundred, attracted people who did not wish to participate in the rapid industrial changes of the first half of the nineteenth century. These communities emphasized consensual over adversarial values.

Until the American Civil War, alternative dispute settlement had expressed an ideology of community cohesion. The Civil War marked a dramatic change from alternatives as an ideology of community justice to alternatives as an external instrument of social control; this change was used as an argument for judicial efficiency, a way of diverting fears of class and racial warfare. The Freedman's Bureau was established to manage the transition from slavery to freedom and the large volume of civil disputes between former masters and newly freed slaves. When, at the close of the nineteenth century, the country's population swelled under unprecedented immigration, new forms of dispute settlement became evident—the padrone system, mediation, conciliation, and so on—and these systems lasted until the new industrial workers became acculturated. Auerbach argues that alternatives arise in almost every generation in an effort to legitimate a legal system that has failed to achieve justice. By 1958, Auerbach contends, the centrality of law in American society was completely established, but once again reformers called attention to problems of access to justice. Two different approaches to reform emerged: one had a populist orientation and ostensibly sought to empower citizens; the other was an offshoot of the legal community itself. Finally, Auerbach concludes that court victories by disadvantaged groups became an incentive for promotion of the new informal justice. The use of alternatives may span a narrow or broad range and become hegemonic control, as becomes clearer in my story of the more recent rise and interpenetration of harmony models intranationally and their spread internationally since the late 1960s. The issue was civil justice.

The 1960s in the United States are described as confrontative because many social groups came forward with their rights agendas: civil rights, consumer rights, women's rights, environmental rights, Native American rights, and more. Law and lawyers were criticized from the political right and left in relation to access to rights and remedies. Mauro Cappelletti, a law professor from Stanford University and the European University at Florence, was an important catalyst in the work on civil litigation, work funded in part by the Ford Foundation. In his general world survey on access problems (1973), Cappelletti concluded that the idea that access to law for workers, ethnics, consumers, and other more generally disenfranchised citizens was an idea whose time was long overdue. The scholarship of this period called for more-democratized access to legal remedy, for making law more accessible to individuals and groups traditionally denied "access to justice." However, Cappelletti and his colleagues were aware that modernizing and streamlining legal systems often destroy what was working as popular and lay justice. The solution to what he called the "legal poverty" of our own cultures was to be found in nonadversarial mechanisms in so-called primitive cultures. The underclass would have informal justice rather than prevention or class action:

aggregate solutions were never part of the picture, nor was the notion of the cumulative effect of empowering plaintiffs.

That one reviewer of Cappelletti's effort (Dill 1981) titled his review essay "Law Reform and Social Inequality: Twentieth-Century Revolution in Civil Justice?" suggests that a change in civil justice might become revolutionary in the broadest sense; but even broader patterns of change in the character of law were yet to come as a result of clashing interests between democracy and plutocracy. Although there was concern about social justice in the 1960s and early 1970s, it is now apparent that over the period of thirty years since the 1970s, the United States moved away from a concern with justice to a concern with harmony and efficiency, from a concern with right and wrong to a concern with therapeutic treatment, from courts to ADR, from law to antilaw ideology. There was also a trend—still continuing—toward the relinquishment of government to private realms. (Note the privatization of prisons and welfare management.) Implicated in this shift was the "access to justice activists," although the initial public thrust came from the judiciary.

Chief Justice Burger led the antilaw campaign at the 1976 Pound conference and thereafter as well. I may have been the only social scientist asked to speak at the conference. At first I was bewildered by the reaction to my comments. In response to the chief justice, who ended his talk by saying, "We need a Henry Ford of the law," I said I thought we needed a mass transit system for the law (i.e., class action). Herman Kahn, of thermonuclear war fame, came up to the podium waving his arms saying, "No, no, mass transit doesn't work." Others were puzzled by my social justice stance amidst efficiency and harmony models. Understanding the implications of the rhetoric at this moment was key to understanding what this gathering of illustrious judges was all about (Nader 1989). The language of the conference was rich with examples of the use of discourse to select, construct, communicate, or obfuscate. The linguistic appeal was to dichotomies and binary thinking—that is, substitutes for arguments based on evidence—and this method of opposing harmony to conflict allowed the advocates of ADR to set up an ideological framework that underlined the virtues of ADR and cast doubt on the search for justice through legal means. The rhetoric extolled the virtues of alternative mechanisms governed by ideologies of harmony and efficiency: American courts were too crowded, and American lawyers and the American people were too litigious; the solutions had to be alternatives to litigation, the multidoor virtuous agencies of settlement or reconciliation. The conference was the launching of a reactionary law reform movement, inhabited by people ranging from the extreme right to liberal persuasions.

After the conference, the public was subjected to an alternative dispute rhetoric, led by the chief justice, that followed a restrictive and formulaic code. In the best tradition of contemporary propaganda, broad generalizations followed patterns of assertive rhetoric that were repetitive, alarming in that they invoked authority and danger, and misleading in that they presented values as facts: the rhetoric claimed that ADR was associated with peace; judicial processes were associated with war; the law and rules of law were complicated and created uncertainties that stimulated feelings of anxiety; law was confrontational, whereas ADR gently and sensitively healed human conflicts and produced only winners and modern, "civilized" citizens. The tone was therapy talk that equated any kind of critical thinking with a "spirit of alienation."

One might indeed conclude that as a result of the effort to repress Vietnam protesters and quell the rights movements of the 1960s, harmony became a virtue in the United States. To be more "civilized," Americans had to abandon the adversary model. Relationships, not root causes, and interpersonal conflict resolution skills not power inequities or injustice, were, and still are, at the heart of ADR. In ADR, civil plaintiffs are perceived as "patients" needing treatment, and when the masses are perceived in this way, policy is invented not to empower the citizen but to treat the patient. There was a movement from an interest in social justice to primary concerns over harmony consensus and efficiency.

The ADR movement attracted strange bedfellows—businesses tired of paying outrageous lawyers' fees, administrators, religious communities, right-wing politicians against the rights agendas, psychotherapy groups, educators, do-gooders, and even 1960s activists. The ADR movement repeated their disaffections: litigation is too costly, too time-consuming, disruptive, uncertain, wasteful, and narrowly focused. Overnight, ADR became an industry, and the movement was institutionalized. The quick expansion of ADR in the United States shows the powerful intervention at the highest levels of the judiciary in promoting it (Nader 1989). But the hegemonic elements of this control are far more pervasive than the direct extension of state control. An intolerance of conflict seeped into the culture; the goal was to prevent not the *causes* of discord but the *expression* of it. By multiple means, the ADR industry attempted to create consensus, homogeneity, agreement, and conformity and to outlaw contentiousness. An expression of candor was seen as an aggressive act, especially in the workplace, on the school playground, and in doctor's office. Even law firms started hiring psychological counselors for outspoken people as the firms also gradually bought into the notion of mediated consensus to manage their workers, while, more surprisingly, lawyers and judges accepted attacks on their profession with equanimity (Nader 1993a). In the early 1990s, with the help of a legal secretary, I investigated two settings in the practice of corporate law. In one instance we described the manner in which corporate lawyers are controlled, and in the other we probed the manner in which nonlawyers working in the same law firm resist coercive harmony. In both instances I was dealing with ongoing ethnographic observations from several large international law firms in the San Francisco Bay Area. Preliminary results were included in Nader 1993a. The law firm culture is an interweaving of hierarchy (Kennedy 1982) and coercive harmony, an interweaving that magnifies habits in that part of the larger culture that fits within the ADR law reform ideology.

ADR: FACTS AND FICTIONS

The critics of ADR sought to separate fact from fiction and in the process to examine assumptions. Marc Galanter of the University of Wisconsin was a leading critic (1993). Galanter and numerous other skeptics found that the United States invests more money in law enforcement than in courts. They found that litigation, as measured by civil funding, had remained relatively stable in the United States, especially when compared with other industrial countries such as Canada and New Zealand and countries in Western Europe, although litigation was more common here than in Japan, Spain, and Italy. The assumption that there had been a litigation explosion was an ideological construct that did not stand up to empirical scrutiny (Nelson 1988). Similarly, assertions that U.S. citizens were contentious people were disproved, although litigation had become a symbolic presence because of the high profile of product liability cases concerning, for example, asbestos, and the Dalkon Shield contraceptive device. In addition, jury awards in product liability cases were not as high as claimed (Vidmar 1992); the criticism leveled against juries in medical malpractice cases did not withstand the empirical gaze. Indeed, data on product liability cases show that such cases make up less than 5 percent of all tort cases in state courts. The number of personal injury cases has actually gone down since 1986, and a study by the American Bar Association found the median punitive damages award to be $30,000. Whether in the work of Abel (1982), Harrington (1985), Hofrichter (1987), Nader (1978), Galanter (1983, 1986, 1993), or Tomasic and Feeley (1982), a question asked was bound to be: By what means was an ADR movement launched in a country where the rule of law was by now so paramount? Galanter gives some indication of why while showing that each litany is false, but in a complicated way:

> Public discussion of our civil justice system resounds with
> a litany of quarter-truths: America is the most litigious so-
> ciety in the course of all human history; Americans sue at
> the drop of a hat; the courts are brimming over with frivo-

lous lawsuits; courts are a first rather than a last resort; run-
away juries make capricious awards to undeserving claim-
ants; immense punitive damage awards are routine;
litigation is undermining our ability to compete economically. (1993: 77)

He concludes with a plea for reform based on adequate knowledge rather than on "a debate dominated by bogus questions
and fictional facts" (77), or partial truths.

Others argued the relative values of settlement and litigation
and asked, What is so good about settlement, or, conversely,
what is so bad about litigation? (Fiss 1984). One need not argue
that the judicial system is perfect, only that its deficiencies have
been falsely portrayed. At the Pound conference, environmen-
tal-, consumer-, and gender-related cases were referred to as
"garbage cases." The argument about a litigation explosion,
concocted by people who were more worried about *who* was
litigating than about the amount of litigation, was an ideological
construct. It began to look very much as if ADR were a pacification scheme, an attempt on the part of powerful interests in
law and in economics to stem litigation by the masses, disguised
by the rhetoric of an imaginary litigation explosion. Unfortunately, those who went along were often unable to distinguish
ADR's psychotherapy-influenced forums from "traditional" legal mediation in the style of Professor Lon Fuller.

ADR practice became institutionalized and examined. Sociologist Judy Rothschild's (1986) study of a neighborhood justice center in San Francisco concluded that the ideology of mediation depends upon a negative evaluation of a traditional legal
system, an evaluation that does not pursue root causes. Dispu-

tants are trained to associate litigation with alienation, hostility, and high cost and to look upon mediation as a process that "encourages" civic and community responsibility for dispute resolution. When disputes are framed as "communication problems," disputes about facts and legal rights become disputes about feelings and relationships. A therapeutic model replaces the legal one, and justice is measured by implicit standards of conformity. Social justice as generally understood (for the good of the whole) then becomes irrelevant.

In 1993, an extended study of popular justice by Sally Merry and Neil Milner appeared, a result of more conferencing. The work pertains to a well-funded San Francisco–based legal alternative, the San Francisco Community Boards (SFCB). The contributors to this study are rather outspoken on some of the issues that Rothschild raised. At the outset, Merry exposes the links between state law and so-called local law or ADR mechanisms. She sees these as constituting a dynamic social field in which mutual influence is the rule. By dismissing the dynamics, the advocates of ADR are able to romanticize it and construct instead a set of ideals that includes a timeless community and peaceful individuals. In analyzing the experience of the SFCB, Yngvesson (1993b: 382) focuses on the "politics involved in the production of an ideology of community empowerment." Instead of questioning the injustices behind the cases, the dispute resolution processes of the SFCB attempt to construct a romantic and idealized view of community in a social environment where structural differences rather than shared values characterize individuals. In a similar vein, Harrington (1993) examines the politics of community conflict resolution in the SFCB. She questions whether mediation is autonomous from the state institutions by portraying the SFCB as a fundamentally conservative form of neopopulism.

In an article titled "When is Popular Justice Popular?" (1993b) in the same volume, I address the presupposition that movements of "popular justice" originate from below. I compare two San Francisco experiments. My argument builds on the observation that popular movements like San Francisco Consumer Action (SFCA) *were* created from below to address the real causes of consumer problems and to provide access to justice, whereas the foundation-funded SFCB, far from dealing with social or individual justice issues, dismissed power differentials and suppressed legal claims in the name of the ideal community.

And finally, Fitzpatrick (1993) unveils the mythological foundations of popular justice in the case of SFCB. He calls the "alternative" disputing process a myth not only because it affirmed itself in opposition to the formal law but because it combined with other equally suspect notions, such as essentialization of formal law, the naturalization of community and individual, the existence of transcendent communal values, and the notion of representation of an invented community. Fitzpatrick eventually rescues the possibility of configuring such law by making visible and clear the values and interests that it shares with formal law. None of these criticisms, nor similar ones made by law professors and social scientists, stemmed the tide of an expanding ADR movement. There was an ADR explosion.

By the early 1990s, in a weird contradiction, ADR became mandatory in many states. People were not flocking to use ADR; they had to be coerced into using it. The movement for voluntary mediation of divorce disputes began several decades ago as lawyers and therapists offered to help clients settle their cases in a nonadversarial manner. In 1991, the late Trina Grillo, a law professor and mediator, published in the influential *Yale Law Journal* a seething critique of mandatory mediation in relation to "process dangers" for women. Central to Grillo's critique was the relation of law to the promises of mediation in family disputes and the "promise" in the form. Mediation promised to take context into account: it would allow room for emotion as well as rationality, and partners would have a say in determining their futures. On the contrary, as Grillo showed, mediation operates as control in defining the problem, limiting speech and expression, and narrowing the public record, since mediation is confidential rather than public. She was most concerned with what happens when mediators frame cases between partners as equals when there is unequal responsibility, and when female anger is suppressed. She concluded that the presumption of equality destroys social context, rights, and especially discussion of fault and limits past the expression of facts in the case. The model that Grillo attacked is less one of law than of therapy: Some conclude that the movement is characterized by forum fetishism, others that it supports soft patriarchy.

Mandatory mediation abridges American freedom because it is often outside the law: it is generally hidden from view, and it eliminates choice of procedure, removes the right to equal protection before an adversary, and furthermore, like psychotherapy, provides for little regulation or accountability. Here again the civil plaintiff becomes a patient, and as Grillo said, mediation becomes a "mutually regulated dance between oppressor and oppressed," a dance that obscures issues of unequal social power. ADR operates as a condition of "moral minimalism," one in which people who dislike confrontation and prefer the least extreme reactions to offenses are reluctant to exercise any social control against one another at all. Moral minimalism, according to M. P. Baumgartner (1988), is found where social interaction is diffuse; it is a result of atomization and transiency in suburbs, for example. Restrained response to grievances is the norm.

In all fairness, it needs to be underscored that the successful institutionalization of ADR required a draw of some sort: even though users were not automatically attracted to it, many other actors were, including large corporations that saw it as a cheaper and faster alternative to the courts. Others, such as the religiously conservative Southern Baptists that Carol Greenhouse studied, found ADR attractive for nonmaterialistic value reasons. The most striking incentive was for those who were either therapists or patients of therapists. Since the latter are widely spread throughout the country, especially on the coasts, this ready-made constituency gave ADR a boost. Two representatives of the therapy community played an important part in the debates over ADR: Deborah Tannen and Daniel Goleman (both, ironically enough, were my students). Tannen, a linguist, has written a number of best-selling books arguing that conflict between men and women results from miscommunication, especially in the workplace. In her book, *The Argument Culture* (1998), Tannen holds that Americans argue too much and litigate too much and we ought to stop arguing and emulate Asian traditions (Asians, by the way, do not have state democratic traditions) that avoid polarization and focus on harmony to manage conflict. Tannen exhibits a skepticism toward democratic deliberation. She admires Japanese management styles, which, while hierarchical, are nevertheless harmonious. Her communitarian view of the world implicitly advocates government by "consensus" rather than democracy.

Daniel Goleman's *Emotional Intelligence* (1996), according to his story in the Harvard alumni magazine (Lambert 1998), has sold over four million copies and is in print in twenty-four languages. This global best-seller preaches self-awareness, emotion management, empathy, teamwork, persuasion, and relationship management. One might call his position Machiavellian or categorize it as a form of conflict prevention. I would prefer to call it a cop-out, an avoidance of root causes by means of human management techniques. The United States went through this same ideological movement at the turn of the century—again pacification—a movement not too far from Roger Fisher's "getting to yes" (1981) through negotiation practices.

THE INTERNATIONALIZATION OF ADR

My first indication that transnational ADR had spread to the international arena came when I was invited to address a workshop for Southeast Asian mediators from places like the Philippines, China, and Thailand, who were brought to the United States to learn about "modern" mediation. I was struck by the absurdity of an American teaching the Chinese how to mediate when mediation was far more traditional and ubiquitous in China than in the United States. The intent of the workshop was to modernize and professionalize mediation in places like China. It occurred to me then that Chinese mediation was different from "modern" mediation and also different from the legal idea of mediation. American ADR has its own cultural baggage in hegemonic characteristics independent of ethnic or legal mediation practices elsewhere. Apparently there was a need to universalize mediation practices.

Shortly after this workshop I decided to examine the way in which alternatives to legal adjudication might have penetrated the negotiation processes in international river disputes (Nader 1995). I had realized that this might be a fruitful avenue for research after having read a manuscript implying that the world's more civilized nations value mediation and negotiation over adjudication, whereas Arab peoples purportedly have not learned to negotiate because they are not yet developed. These value-laden statements caught my attention because earlier scholarship in anthropology and sociology had ranked dispute resolution techniques on a scale that ranged from self-help to negotiation to mediation to arbitration and finally to adjudication on the most "civilized" end of the scale. Nineteenth-century legal scholars considered the existence of law courts to be a sign of a people's social complexity and modernity. Indeed, colonial powers regarded the introduction of courts in Africa as part of the civilizing mission, and the International Court of Justice was promoted as the apex of forums for the settlement of international disputes by means of adjudication and arbitration. The popularity of ADR as policy in the 1980s and 1990s signified a paradoxical switch from the more civilized processes of dispute resolution to "softer," nonadversarial means such as mediation or negotiation.

It appears that the ranked preferences for dispute-handling forums do reflect the distribution of international power. As "less civilized" nations achieve what was once the hallmark of civilization, law courts, a new standard for civilization, mediation, replaces the old. As one international legal scholar pointed out "The less 'civilized' were doomed to work toward an equality which an elastic standard of 'civilization' put forever beyond their reach....the 'civilized' had a way of becoming more 'civilized' still" (Gong 1984: 63). Just as ADR in the United States moved the rhetoric from justice to harmony, so too at the international level has the notion of "mature" negotiation, conceived as the "standard of civilized behavior," been replacing the World Court. Why this international valorizing of negotiation? Edward Said (1978) acknowledged in his notion of "flexible positional superiority" that the valorization of one cultural form over another is frequently linked to imbalances in power: once the "primitives" had courts, we moved to international negotiations or ADR.

Not only were mediation and negotiation valorized, but American ADR was thought to be cross-culturally usable. Avruch and Black (1996) have demonstrated how ADR is being exported to Pacific countries like Palau without consideration of cultural patterns. And if you do not believe that these processes are culturally interchangeable, the ADR experts might add, read Philip Gulliver's cross-cultural work *Disputes and Negotiations* (1963): Gulliver, they say, proved that mediation and negotiation were universalistic. Indicative of underlying political interests, the Palau operation aimed to establish easy tools of social control: "Concentrating on individual remedies...neglects macrostructural questions of power and inequality" (Avruch and Black 52). The commodification and export of ADR are real. Commercial interests are linked to political goals of the United States government, which funds these attempts. The same may be said of the "legal imperialism" implicit in the export of ADR to the Eastern bloc in the name of democratization.

The International Court of Justice, the major tribunal for international law, was founded upon the precedents of the Permanent Court of International Justice, which had been a part of the League of Nations. Currently, the court at the Hague operates under statute as part of the United Nations charter organized after World War II. Fifteen independent judges are elected by the Security Council and the General Assembly of the United Nations to integrate the court. Since the United States joined the court in 1946, there have been important changes in its composition and in the types of cases it considers. After the emergence of new nations, many of them Third World, the older standard of adjudication and arbitration in the World Court apparently became less useful to the more powerful nations when they noted the new nations' readiness to use the court to represent new national interests on equal terms with the old. The influence of the Third World in the court began to take effect after 1964, when there were a number of rulings in favor of Third World and postcolonial states. In 1966 the court ruled in favor of Liberian and Ethiopian plaintiffs and against South Africa; in 1974, for New Zealand and Australia and against France. In 1984 Nicaragua filed suit against the United States, which withdrew from the case and shortly thereafter withdrew from the agreement of voluntary compliance with court decisions. Both the Soviet Union, in the mid-1960s, and the United States, in the mid-1980s, withheld dues, evincing a position of indifference to international law.

Some noticed that the court's clientele was vanishing (Franck 1986).

Under the stimulus of ADR, the United States turned instead toward international negotiation teams drawn from a new professional class of negotiators and mediators from the fields of law, economics, social psychology, political science, and psychotherapy—few came from anthropology. What was new about these negotiators was not that they were practicing mediation or negotiation—after all, such modes of dispute processing had been around for a long time. What they had in common was a distaste for confrontational adversarial processes, for courts as a way to handle the problems of the masses, for justice over compromise.

Those who write about the emerging system of international negotiations totally ignore the World Court and focus instead on the functions of a system of negotiation: that system should contribute to the stability and growth of the system of international relations. For such people, international conflict no longer involves government-to-government negotiation but rather international cooperation between governments negotiating in the name of stability. Certainly international stability may be a good thing, but it can also mean injustice and continuing inequities that in the long run promote more instability. The overall implication in much of this Euro-American literature is that anything can and should be negotiated to keep peace. Yet not everyone agrees. The failure to address inequities often leads to the opposite of peace—war and violence. The negotiation model has a serious flaw if it is cast as the only avenue and not part of an appeals structure—instead of being adjudicated in the international court, disputes are to be settled by "mutual learning," "information sharing," "harmonizing," and "cooperation"; zero-sum settlements become "hostile," and information, analysis, and solution get in the way of "constructive dialogue." There is a psychologizing of phenomena that have nothing to do with the psyche and a great deal to do with power relations formed by means of intense influencing. Under such conditions, mind games become a central component of this ADR negotiation process: for example, in international negotiations over rivers, toxic poisoning is referred to as a "perception of toxic poisoning," and new questions are asked, such as "How can cultural behavior be used or neutralized?" Negotiation in this style becomes manipulation of water disputes pure and simple.

My initial survey of water resource disputes[5] indicates the transition of dispute resolution forums suggested earlier, away from adjudication or arbitration and toward negotiation. In the case of the Danube River Basin, a clear example, the progression moves temporally from (1) procedures of international adjudication or arbitration to (2) basinwide planning, whereby river basin commissions deal cooperatively to (3) bilateral agreements resulting from international bargaining to (4) the operation of nongovernmental organizations across political and bureaucratic boundaries. Such transitions strikingly mirror both the

---

5. Water resource conflicts have serious consequences. They lead to mass migration, peasant revolts, and urban insurrection. Officials from the Department of Defense, the CIA, the State Department, and the White House discussed these issues when they met in September 1999 to study the global implications of water conflicts. Futurists are already predicting water wars.

"privatization" of justice through ADR centers in the United States and the growth of large private organizations exercising government powers.

The Danube is one of the most international river basins in the world, touching eight countries and more than seventy million people. The rich upper riparians use the Danube primarily for industry, waste disposal, and energy. The lower riparians use the river for drinking water, irrigation, fisheries, tourism, and other nonindustrial purposes. Joanne Linneroth, the author who synthesized the Danube case, implies that there *is* a "universal negotiating culture," or what she calls a "common culture," consisting of national governmental administrators, international scientific communities, and emerging environmental groups; and she calls for win-win bargaining by those who share "a certain professional rationality" who will "translate the order, its imagery, and social expectations": in short, she calls for the privatizing of international justice. The language she uses to describe how conflicting, adversarial interests might be negotiated reveals the influence of therapy: "mutual learning" and "information sharing" sound more like marital therapy terms than terms to be applied to conflicts over river pollution (Linneroth 1990: 637, 658–59).

When therapy talk is strong, there is little consideration of the causes of disputes that *are* in their effects zero-sum. Nor is there acknowledgment that bilateral negotiation may give the stronger nation a bargaining advantage over the weaker nation. Indeed, in this view, anything can be negotiated, even if "perceptions" must first be molded and shifted away from "information, analysis, and solution" to mechanisms for "constructive dialogue." What is claimed to be universal is a hegemonic perspective on disputing. The most recent hegemony, encapsulated in a harmony ideology developed in the United States during the 1970s, has now been exported worldwide. It has a coercive strain whose primary function is, I believe, pacification. Two international lawyers put it this way:

> At a time when the forces of law and order need ever increasing recognition in the international arena, the notion that states willing to submit international river disputes to adjudication are ill advised has a strange ring indeed.. . . the cry of inadequacy of courts. . .betrays a nostalgia for a fast-fading conception of international law in which naked power holds greater sway than recognized principles of justice. (Laylin and Bianchi 1959: 49)

In case after case, the weaker party looks to adjudication while the stronger party prefers to negotiate. The Douro River in Spain is another case in point (Dellapenna 1992). A proposed nuclear waste facility at Aldeavilla in Spain will be less than one kilometer from Portugal, and any contamination of the Douro River will end up in Portugal. Seventy percent of Portugal's surface freshwater comes from rivers that rise in Spain, whereas Spain receives virtually none of its surface freshwater from Portugal. Portugal's weak position would not bode well for a fair bilateral settlement because of the freshwater power differential between the two nations and because Spain is already clearly violating customary international law by threatening the flow of fresh water to its neighbor.

The Valle de Mexicali, one of the richest agricultural regions in Mexico, is another case. There the protest is over an all-

American plan to limit groundwater leakage that Mexico needs to support its crops. Americans plead (Hayes 1991) for the use of negotiation so that a win-win solution is possible, and they chide Mexican officials for threatening international litigation in the World Court, saying "Such a development goes against the grain of ordered, controlled, international management of resources." There is no hint that international tribunals would act rationally, logically, and humanely.

The Jordan River case in the Middle East is more complex, involving Lebanon, Jordan, Israel, and Syria and gross inequities in the consumption of water. Four tributaries of the Jordan are involved. The Dan River, which originates in pre-1967 Israel, discharges into the upper Jordan, as do the Hasbani River, which originates in southern Lebanon, and the Banias River, which originates in the Syrian Golan Heights. The Yarmouk River, which forms the border between Syria and Jordan, discharges into the lower Jordan. During the middle 1950s, the attempts of Eric Johnston, the United States ambassador to Jordan, to devise several water allocation plans led to the Unified Plan. This plan was formally accepted by the parties involved, but for domestic political reasons they made no permanent commitments. Unilateral actions followed, and eventually it was Israel, after occupying the Golan Heights and the West Bank in 1967, that gained real control over the Jordan headwaters and the Yarmouk River. Soon after the 1967 occupation of the West Bank, the Israeli authorities started a rationing program that by the 1990s gave four times as much water per capita to Israeli settlers as to Arabs, requiring the latter to seek permission to drill wells. The situation went from mediated negotiations to unilateral action to violent conflict, and an adjudicated settlement was never considered. Some attribute the *Intifadah* grievances to the economic effects of water scarcity.

The long-standing Ganges River dispute between Bangladesh and India is yet another clear example of the politics of international negotiation and the advantages of bilateral negotiation for the stronger party. After a series of failed negotiations, the government of Bangladesh tried to bring its case before the United Nations General Assembly. India objected, arguing that the Farakka Barrage dam was a "bilateral issue." India could get moral support for its unilateral action, while Bangladesh, one of the poorest countries in the world, had little clout in the international arena. According to Khurshida Begum (1988: 204–14), peaceful negotiation, strictly bilateral, is a hegemonic tool for India. Over the course of the negotiations, "discrepancies" between the facts reported by the two countries revealed the very reason for which court trials are useful— disagreements of fact. Of course, the serious effects of water shortage claimed by Bangladesh would seem to put this case, like that of Palestinians in Israel, on the level of human rights violations.

There is a stridency to all these objections to the World Court, particularly among those who supported the policies of the United States in Central America in the 1980s. Whether such instances actually caused the trend toward privatization of international river disputes is hard to say, but there was most certainly a realignment of the principles grounding international law toward the older view "in which naked power holds greater sway than recognized principles of justice" (Laylin and Bianchi 1959: 49). It might also be noted that although the

scholarly literature on globalization is immense, only a minuscule part of that literature deals with law and its larger purposes. That the literature is limited was indicated by an initial
overview in 1994 by David Trubek and others and one in 1996
by Dezalay and Garth (1996). Dezalay and Garth applied the
framework of competition to business disputes; they used the
market model. Emerging competition between mediator tech-
nicians and judges and the blurring of the boundaries between
negotiation, mediation, and arbitration led them to conclude
that "to date the domestic ADR movement has had relatively
little success internationally"! (151–52).

TRADE IDEOLOGY
AND HARMONY IDEOLOGY

Before concluding, I would like to mention my very cursory
overview of the relationships or possible congruencies between
trade ideology and harmony ideology. Much of the language is
similar—both use terms like "negotiate," "strike a deal," and
so on—and we might remember that trade, according to classic
liberal theory, is a "win-win" transaction. General Agreement
on Tariffs and Trade is an interesting case in need of ethnographic examination.

The agreement emerged in the years immediately following
World War II in response to two schools of thought that spearheaded the movement toward a global trade organization (Jackson 1989). One group thought that such an organization would
create economic growth through expanded trade. A second
thought that an international trade organization would promote global stability and prevent war. In 1947, GATT was

drawn up in Geneva with the expectation that a formal international organization, the International Trade Organization (ITO), would oversee its implementation. Periodically, GATT sponsored "rounds," or major sets of negotiations. Besides tariff questions, recent rounds have addressed the question of dispute settlement procedures.

Both the ITO and GATT were conceived during a time in which the "rule of law" was held up as the most highly evolved forum for settling disputes. These were the years of the fledgling United Nations and the newly established International Court of Justice. A number of U.S. officials who were involved in drafting the ITO charter and GATT seemed strongly committed to the rule-of-law principle, contemplating effective use of arbitration and, in some circumstances, even appeal to the World Court. As with the World Court, the entry of dozens of postcolonial nations into GATT in the early 1960s prompted a different attitude toward the settlement of disputes, and the literature on the shift away from legality and toward pragmatism is extensive. "Conciliation" was the term used to describe GATT activities between 1963 and 1970, when adjudication was dormant; and this term continued to be used until the 1980s, when expert panels increased in popularity. By the late 1980s, most nations seemed to indicate a preference for the implementation of more-legalistic procedures. The power of the World Trade Organization (WTO, the successor to GATT) resides in its dispute resolution panels, which allow any WTO member country to challenge privately the *domestic* laws of any other member without media observers. The Seattle WTO protests in the fall of 1999 may be a good example of how nondemocratic forums can put a lid on explosive situations by not being more open to the public.

There is a certain irony to the fact that just as GATT swings to a more "rules-based" approach (which would conceivably bode well for the less developed countries), alternative trading arrangements like NAFTA are formed. In the WTO, we see an international class of negotiators and technocrats shaping policy for an international class of corporations through international trading arrangements—a phenomenon some have called the strangulation of national sovereignty by the rein of multinationals. The WTO itself has its own training school in Geneva to teach the international negotiating culture to prospective negotiators from new member states. Some speak seriously about the manufacturing of consensus (Ikenberry 1989). That once again anthropological work is invoked as scientific justification indicates the necessity for further inquiry into the unending influence of the soft technologies of dispute resolution on globalization. Both adversarial law models and harmony law models play an important part in globalization strategies, but of the two, harmony law models of the ADR type are the least attended to in theoretical discussion.

Saskia Sassen (1995) argues that there is no global law. Rather, there is a regime of international law characterized by the hegemony of neoliberal concepts of economic relations very much in the American style; international arbitration and the new specialty in conflict resolution are key legal mechanisms of control. Vandana Shiva (1997), in speaking about the new regimes, questions the Eurocentric legal notions of property, which when employed provide the license to the piracy that she sees as the basis for the intellectual property laws of GATT and the WTO. Shiva's critique is searing. For her, there is continuity in globalization of a Western sort: colonialism, development, and "free trade"—meaning, that is, contemporary globalization. Both Sassen and Shiva recognize legal innovations as central vehicles that allow enormous corporate structures to centralize power. The continuities Shiva sees in history I see as well. The shifts from one type of disputing style to another are never total or "evolutionary"; instead, they indicate how elastic models of dispute management are. Elastic arrangements in dispute resolution are often pursued to strengthen the advantage of the stronger bargaining partner, a point to remember.

Since they were created in 1994, the Uruguay Round Agreements have constrained the ability of governments to maintain public interest regulations. These agreements are enforced through the freestanding WTO tribunal system, whose job is to judge countries' laws for WTO compliance. WTO committees and panels meet in secrecy in Geneva, Switzerland, unlike U.S. domestic courts and other international arbitration committees, which are open to the public. Judgments over key areas like food safety or ownership of local knowledge, such as a particular seed variety, can force farmers to pay annual royalties or to buy new seeds each year. The WTO uses automatically binding dispute mechanisms to enforce its trade rules. Once a WTO tribunal has declared a country's law WTO-illegal, the country must change its laws or face trade sanctions. The authority for setting domestic policy is shifting from democratically elected bodies, like the U.S. Congress, to WTO tribunals. The Dispute Resolution Understanding (DSU) has one specific operating rule: all panel activities are confidential. There is no due process, no citizen participation, no outside appeal. WTO disputes are heard by three panelists nominated for each dispute.[6] The WTO is not just about trade but about a reconfiguration of international, national and local law, politics, cultures and values (Wallach and Forza 1999). The centralization of commerce and, with it, the removal of decision making from citizen control was the ultimate in faceless dispute resolution and undoubtedly fueled the opposition in Seattle in November 1999 and others since.

When Vandana Shiva uses the term "biopiracy," she is referring to the commercial appropriation of plants, seeds, and traditional processes for obtaining medicinal plants. The most famous example of biopiracy involves patents on products taken from the neem tree, a native to India, nicknamed "the village pharmacy." W. R. Grace & Company has started manufacturing its own neem products, for which it carries a patent on an "innovation" based on traditional knowledge. Under the WTO Agreement on Trade-Related Aspects of Intellectual Property Rights (TRIPs), W. R. Grace is defending itself against the Indian challenge to the company's patent claim. Similar challenges have been made in Thailand.

A GRADUAL EROSION

Distinguished Western scholars of the past—Weber, Durkheim, Maine—were interested in the challenging broad ques-

---

6. WTO Understanding on Rules and Procedures Governing the Settlement of Disputes (DSU), Article 14 and Appendix 3, Paragraphs 2 and 3.

tions of law. In this century, they might ask What is the character of law? What are the broad patterns of change that have appeared at the onset of the twenty-first century? Or why is legal precedence being disappeared by means of depublishing or decertifying legal opinions? It appears that the ADR twentieth-century revolution in civil justice is less a legal innovation concerned with social inequalities of the 1960s and early 1970s than a movement away from justice toward harmony and efficiency models. The political concerns of the left and the right have converged to transform dispute resolution from the rule of law to the rule of coercion by economists and therapists. By manipulating multiculturalism, a dispute resolution model appears to be unfractured by power differences and increasingly originating from multinational institutions. The justice motive is being replaced by harmony and is explained by one anthropologist as "imperialist nostalgia" (Rosaldo 1989) or the need to consume that which has been destroyed—community; and efficiency is justified by the market. The two—nostalgia and the marketplace—go hand in hand.

Ellen Hertz (1991) is convincing in arguing that, while the Chicago School of economics has not come to dominate antitrust law entirely, it has—under the false assumption that market information is equally available to all—effected a basic shift in the kinds of questions that count and that lawyers therefore feel are relevant to antitrust analyses. Meanwhile, at Harvard Law School, also under the influence of economists—namely, game theory economists—and harmony mediation ideology, the Program on Negotiation was launched. I am well aware of its effect, nationally and internationally, on the style of conflict management, under the influence of Professor Roger Fisher's "getting to yes" negotiation philosophy. If we add the language of "costs," "benefits," "trade-offs," and "optimal mixes" to these two transformative sources, we have the ingredients for a technocratic hegemony. There are consequences that flow from these paradigm revolutions.

In the United States, workers are losing the right to sue. Newspaper articles seriously suggest that corporate presidents who commit grave antitrust violations should not go to prison because it is more efficient to fine them (they have the money) and allow them to continue as productive members of the corporate community. Serious arguments are made for equal treatment of parties who are not equal and for the reinvention of indigenous law in the midst of international arms dealing and natural-resource plundering.[7] We begin to see in a number of seemingly unrelated sites the same phenomenon—an antilaw movement. The access-to-law movement was the revolt against legal formalism and went much further than the legal realists' instrumentalism might have wished. But, whereas Roscoe Pound felt that "social control is primarily the function of the state and is exercised through law," state law is being taken over by harmony and efficiency paradigms. As with the law-against-law conflict encountered by the legal development movement, legal instrumentalism frequently undermines legal formalism and the rule of law and leaves instrumental law at the disposal of users, or authoritarian ordering. Abroad, as well

7. Again I recommend the thoughtful article by von Benda-Beckmann, "Citizens, Strangers, and Indigenous Peoples: Conceptual Politics and Legal Pluralism" (1997). He quotes a Maori who radically rejects "legal pluralism" because it maintains the dishonesty of illusion.

as at home, hegemonic processes in law have had their impact.

The question, Why do Zapotecs talk about harmony while litigating like crazy? took me away from a small village in Mexico and into an examination of the meaning of Christian colonization in Africa, Latin America, Fiji, New Guinea, and the United States. *Harmony Ideology* was my dialogue between views I see as opposing one another but occupying a continuum in controlling processes. My work combines inductive and deductive perspectives and involves historical, interpretive, ethnographic, and comparative approaches as well. It is an eclectic methodology, one that is driven by the questions and by the desire for holistic understanding and situating of the justice motive.

A study of the uses of harmony as control led me from a particularistic ethnography dealing with styles of disputing to a broader cultural analysis of a style of religion in politics that Americans saw elaborated in a postconfrontational politics in the 2000 U.S. elections. The cultural study of harmony control has taken me and my students into workplaces, dormitories, mental health settings, classrooms, and African villages, as well as law firms—places where harmony ideology is increasingly commonplace, where conflict may be thought of as principally due to communication problems, or where contention is questioned. I am also moved to inquire whether and how the American-originated ADR movement has spread internationally to rekindle or to replace older mechanisms, as in international river disputes, and to form the basis for dispute management in international trade agreements such as NAFTA and GATT and organizations such as the WTO.

We have come far from the position that derides the study

of disputing as peripheral to the anthropology of law or to law in general. It may be that disputing mechanisms are a key concept for law in society research and a key concept for anthropological theory more generally for reasons I stated in 1965: that is, disputing is ubiquitous, and forums for disputing are prime locales for influence peddling because people care about them. And people care enough about disputing so that even in situations of overwhelming odds, the popular imagination of subordinates allows them to believe and to act as if the existing dominance can be reversed. Although academic theories indicate the opposite and academic pessimism warns against the illusion of legal rights, users of law believe there may be a direct connection between litigation and remedies. For users, disputing carries the possibility of locating their interests within the dominant hegemony; in Gramscian terms disputing serves to articulate an alternative hegemony. Alan Hunt is correct in noting that the "cumulative connections between the elements of micro-politics...are essential if the counter-hegemony is to succeed in displacing an existing hegemony bloc" (1990: 311). It comes as no surprise then that both intention and agency are central to the life of the law.

FOUR

The Plaintiff
A User Theory

Often enough a trouble-case can have an effect like that of a
stone flung into an over-chilled fiord, and set off sudden
crystallization over an area vastly wider than was aimed at or
thought about beforehand.

Karl Llewellyn and E. A. Hoebel

If there be no official voicer of rebuke, much that deserves
rebuke goes thus unrebuked.

Karl Llewellyn and E. A. Hoebel

While the movement of law, whether progressive or retrogres-
sive, may be influenced by scholarly frames of reference such
as elitism or populism or instrumentalism, motion in the law
may also be a result of political transformations such as those
brought about by colonialism, religious missionization, independence movements, global legal imperialism, and borderless
multinational economies. The focus of the earlier chapters

reflected an interest in documenting extensive historical processes as part of the ethnographic project to contextualize these processes and imbue them with meaning. In particular, the harmony legal model emerged as a powerful mode of control, presumably averting adversarial relations and showcasing reconciliatory posturing.

In this last chapter, I elaborate on a number of additional ideas that have proved critical for understanding the dynamics of law in everyday life. The first idea stems from the belief that the search for justice is both fundamental and universal in human culture and society, and a "reflex-like" response to an injustice is often so strong that all other considerations are of secondary importance. This observation implies that forums for justice must be ubiquitous, as indeed they are (Nader and Sursock 1986), even though some people, like the Koreans, are said to prefer peace to justice (Hahm 1969: 44). Notions of justice are implicit in every culture and usually operate at the unconscious and semiconscious levels, becoming explicit only when an injustice is confronted. The second idea is that styles of law vary, even within the same place, in relation to the social and cultural environment, whether hegemonic or not (see, e.g., Aubert 1969; Nader 1969a; Nader and Todd 1978). As a Sard shepherd points out, "If somebody steals my flock, he steals my flock. He does not offend me. It depends, depending on who he is, he offends me, and how he steals, and why" (Nader and Todd 1978: 34). The third and final idea, which I have already introduced—a user theory of law—is that the direction of law is dependent in large measure on who is motivated to use the law and for what purposes. The role of political ideas and influence in regulating access for potential users—the plaintiffs—

and in enlarging legal relevance directs our attention to the larger noble purposes of the law.

Nearly all these ideas are now a part of the research literature on law across the legal and social sciences. I was introduced to the justice motive and how it works through the work of social psychologists (Lerner 1975, 1980; Lerner and Lerner 1981). The idea that law varies with changes in the social and cultural environment has been part of anthropology at least since Sir Henry Maine (1861) postulated that with changes in family structures, the law shifts from being based on one's status to being rooted in contracts between individuals. The specific idea that law varies with modes of social control is found in Elizabeth Colson's work in Africa (1953), in Beatrice Whiting's work on Painte sorcery (1950), and in the work of others mentioned above; and the idea that law varies with status has been extensively pursued by sociologist Donald Black (1976).

The integrative notion that users of law make or create law is my own elaboration on Edward Sapir's work on linguistic drift (1921: 155). Here I paraphrase Sapir on linguistic drift directly rather than attempt to translate Llewellyn's somewhat garbled version of the concept of drift and how it works. The drift of a legal system consists in the users' unconscious selection of individual variations whose effects are cumulative in some specific direction. This direction may be inferred, in the main, from the past history of the system. In the long run, any new feature of the drift becomes part and parcel of the common, accepted law, but for long periods of time the new feature may exist as a mere tendency in the legal system. As we look about us and observe current usage, we may not realize that our legal system has a "slope," that the changes of the next few years are in a sense prefigured in certain obscure tendencies of the present, and that these changes, when consummated, will be seen to be but continuations of changes that have already been initiated. Along these lines, historian Richard Kagan's (1981) work on Spain illuminates the processes whereby numbers and kinds of users expand and contract with changing political and economic conditions, or may also be reframed by new ideologies or charismatic cultural paradigms.

My perspective here is actor oriented—that is, plaintiff oriented in the context of controlling processes working in and beyond law, processes that are usually latent rather than manifest and hence inherently powerful. As I indicate further on, the very possibility that the cases brought by potential users can change everyday life by means of law (e.g., tort cases involving asbestos, the Dalkon Shield, and breast implants) may have generated the present antilaw movements, such as tort "reform," emanating from powerful ideologies as well as from political and economic interest groups in the United States and other points of origin, groups that see benefit in curbing access to litigation.

THE CHANGING ROLE
OF THE PLAINTIFF

In the late 1970s, in a paper titled "The Direction of Law and the Development of Extra-Judicial Processes in Nation-State Societies" (Nader 1978), I elaborated on the argument that the court systems that are part of the court-use patterns of the nation-state apparatus can be manipulated by the state indirectly through administrative means. The direction of law is connected to the development of extrajudicial processes in nation-state societies. For example, judges have pushed ADR as an alternative to adjudication. In addition, states directly block access to courts for particular kinds of lawsuits, such as class action suits. In nation-state societies, the state defines itself as a user by becoming the plaintiff in criminal cases, while the "true" plaintiffs become victims. The rise of nation-states accompanied this historical change from plaintiff to victim, from an active to a passive role, and also changed the status of the defendant as an object of state action. Most defendants in criminal cases are members of the underclass, because individual members of the underclass do not have the power to criticize and resist the definitions of crime and because rulers justify such tendencies as needed to reduce disorder that could result from feuding, for example. We know also that what is considered criminal does change over time and that the political and economic forces behind the creation of criminal law are revealed in history (Chambliss 1982) and in culture and society (Nader and Todd 1978; Nader 2001).

I have also examined the idea that a change in relationships between litigants can trigger behavioral change inside the courtroom (Nader 1985). The plaintiff has gradually moved from a position of relative power in community courts, which allowed for face-to-face disputes (as, for example, in seventeenth-century and eighteenth-century New England villages), to a relatively powerless role that allows room for complaining only in the context of face-to-faceless disputes. The new role of the consumer as complainant rather than disputant in the global marketplace not only is relatively anonymous but may be noticed by the absence of the consumer voice. Changes in the potential litigant role seem to have followed the change in relations that came with the industrialized wage-labor system, as well as with elongation of the product distribution chain and, currently, the globalization of such changes.

As consumers became distanced from producers, the former lost both the power of informal social control, through public opinion for example, and formal social control, such as access to state law. There was no place for "little injustices," which might not be so inconsequential. The result was a decrease in meaningful confrontation in the courtroom and an increase in unilateral behavior—such as complaining or exiting and "lumping it," that is, not doing anything. Eventually, the plaintiff role atrophied because it became monopolized by the state. The law drifted in the direction of its dominant users (Nader 1983: 91)—in this instance, the state or the world of corporations or both.

If the individual plaintiff had indeed been gradually removed from litigation with the rise of nation-states, then my next research priority was to explore further the concept of user itself. I specifically focused attention on the plaintiff in order to loosen the grip that a judge-determined court has on academic concepts of law (as in the frequent conceptualizing of "judicial decision making"). Replacing the picture of a judge-determined law with an interactive model, a user theory of law, gives equal sociological significance to all the players in the litigation process and thereby corrects for transparent disciplinary biases (Nader 1984b).

If we looked at the behavioral sciences and asked where each science has traditionally focused its attention, we would most likely notice that political scientists have generally favored look-

ing at the role of the judge and the hierarchy of judicial decision-making. Sociologists and criminologists have been attentive to the criminal defendant, and psychologists and
anthropologists have focused on the victim or on the plaintiff.
And although anthropologists have looked at interaction between all the parties to a case, including the parties' networks,
few have examined larger historic processes, that is, the evolution of these roles over time.

In nonstate societies of the sort traditionally studied by anthropologists, the plaintiff is motivated to secure justice, and a
certain kind of justice, because he or she is plaintiff as well as
victim. This observation is often ignored when Western law is
transplanted elsewhere, although the implantation of Western
law models has been the cause of major unrest in developing
nations around the world. In Zambia, for instance, the state as
plaintiff began punishing defendants convicted of cattle rustling
by sentencing them to jail, whereas under traditional law, compensation, not punishment, is a central interest for the "true"
individual plaintiffs (Canter 1978). In such situations, plaintiff
energy is frustrated. In the Zambian instance, the frustration
caused major riots and precipitated a local demand that cattle
rustlers be tried by the local court rather than taken out of the
community. *It is in the role of the active plaintiff that litigation in
other societies differs from ours.* In Sardinia, cattle theft is regarded not as a crime but as a dispute that should be settled
without resort to the state (Ruffini 1978). In both Zambia and
Sardinia, the state views the plaintiffs as lawless; the plaintiffs
view the state as unresponsive at the least, more likely as cor-
rupt. Because the key actors vary cross-culturally, an interactive
model that takes all participants into account is imperative for

any valid user theory of law. If the users studied reflect the array of possible users, it follows that everyday life can theoretically be made and changed by the cumulative efforts of users of law.

Just what group constitutes the "users" of law is significant because when the actual law users reflect a broad spectrum of society, the larger culture can be transformed by their efforts in the courtroom; if the spectrum remains narrow, nothing changes. Using United States historical legal data, Willard Hurst (1981) noticed that although there have been changes over the nineteenth and twentieth centuries in what people have chosen to litigate and changes in procedural style, in another sense there has been no significant change at all—the users have not changed: "Nineteenth-century litigation involved only limited sectors of the society in any bulk" (420). With the exception of New Deal administrative agencies, "there are today no more merchants suing fellow merchants in court than there were in the nineteenth-century dockets, and people of small means were not often plaintiffs except in torts or family matters" (421). I should note, however, that if users of courts themselves have tended not to change much in the United States even under conditions of rapid social transformation, then the 1960s were unusual; in the 1960s, cases involving Blacks, Hispanics, Native Americans, consumer groups, environmentalist workers, and women began to push their way into litigation. Some of this litigation involved class action suits.

Before proceeding further, I should like to say again that, contrary to popular representation, Americans go to great lengths *not* to litigate. The Harvard School of Public Health reports that fewer patients bring claims in medical malpractice than are entitled to do so. The same is true for serious product defects. Lumping it is more common than claiming (Felstiner, Abel, and Sarat 1980/81). But when new faces with new cases did begin to exercise their rights as civil plaintiffs in the late 1960s, the alarms went off among powerful potential defendants.

In 1985, in a piece on the Mexican Zapotec entitled "A User Theory of Legal Change as Applied to Gender," I mentioned a work titled *Drinking, Homicide, and Rebellion in Colonial Mexican Villages* (Taylor 1979). In this work, William Taylor discussed gender in relation to litigating parties because in eighteenth-century Oaxaca an unusually high proportion of plaintiffs were women—wives, sex partners, and sex rivals— a proportion higher than that among non-Indians. Taylor's point was that in colonial Mexican villages, violence was restricted to the forum in which it was least likely to turn into village factionalism. The family unit in rural Mexico at the end of the colonial period was significant in productive and reproductive terms, but it was the community that was regarded as the fundamental unit. Taylor argues that conflict focused on women to maintain autonomy and to ensure self-protection among Indian communities. The overall pattern then of violent households and relatively peaceful communities Taylor connects to the political setting. It behooved Indians to tolerate conjugal violence and stress the primacy of the community as a way to avoid having the power of the state weigh in on a disputatious village.

The users in Oaxaca that I observed from 1959 to 1969—a decade of great social change, including out-migration and the opening up of the Zapotec mountain area by a network of roads and airstrips—exhibited little change in their use of the courts. The 409 cases I collected from the village courts—the *presidente, síndico,* and *alcalde* courts—did not yet reflect the behavior of law as shifting as a result of changes in the sociocultural environment. Although Zapotec men and women used the courts for different purposes, the numbers of male and female plaintiffs were about equal. Women made extensive use of the courts to obtain their domestic rights and, as they put it, "to make the balance" in a public forum.

In the Mexican study, I discerned that the interests of the local community with regard to its citizens were different from the interests of the wider society vis-à-vis those same citizens. It seemed evident that the powerholders in the community and in the state system used their power to achieve their respective goals by encouraging free access to the courts at the community level or by permitting only limited access at the state level. In addition, the rank of men relative to women and to one another affected whether and how gender influenced user patterns. It has been observed that throughout the history of Mexico the process of Mexicanization or, more generally, Westernization has often meant a change in the status of Indian men and women; women lose status relative to their menfolk, and men lose status relative to men in the dominant society. Mexican state law may be said to have a bias against defendants, who are primarily men. Village law has a bias toward plaintiffs, who are both male and female. The state, it appears, restricts the plaintiff role, and males monopolize the defendant role.

On the other hand, my examination of cross-sex court cases showed that the styles used varied by the type of case, from accusatory to compensatory, remedial, and penal. Paternity cases were accusatory, and all the plaintiffs demanded compensation. Cases in which women asked for divorce or separation to escape physical abuse were almost always transformed into conciliatory, compensatory, or remedial action. In cases of abandonment, adultery, and abortion, the style was clearly penal, and the goal was to punish. This range of styles within one community showed clearly that the use patterns of women plaintiffs had a great deal to do with court style. It seemed possible that if family cases were dropped from the docket, the dominant style might be penal.

In a previous study of two distinct Mexican indigenous communities, one in Oaxaca, the other in Chiapas, Duane Metzger and I argued that choices in agencies to remedy conflict are linked to patterns of authority (Nader and Metzger 1963). For example, in Oaxaca, when traditional marriages arranged by family elders were replaced by free-choice marriages and when patterns of early inheritance and the neolocal pattern of residence became commonplace, women's complaint pattern changed from seeking redress within the family to seeking it in a public forum. The responsibility lost or abandoned by the family was then assumed by the community and the state, something that had not yet happened in the Chiapas community.

It is clear that numbers do not tell the whole story about court use, although they are useful. The point is that the types of cases that appear on the docket are patterned, which indicates that law not only controls but is controlled by cultural forces. Court use is interactive rather than simply impositional; it is created by citizen interest rather than solely by town officials.

The situation fits a share-power theory of law, even though the distribution of that power is variable and dynamic.

On the one hand, village law does not differentiate between public and private. On the other hand, at the Oaxaca district court level, there is an impositional model in which the state determines what cases it will hear. Court use by community members is commonly generated by dissatisfaction with hearings in the community court. Mexican state law, in which the state is the plaintiff, has a bias against criminal defendants, most of whom are men, and the state also restricts what arguments or even what cases it will accept from a plaintiff. District courts have managed to settle criminal cases because the state denies village court jurisdiction over matters dealing with serious bodily injury, among other things. The state clearly frustrates the justice motive at the district level, although the exact cause of dissatisfaction at that level differs from that in the community courts. Within any population there is differential justice motivation, but Rincóneros have now learned to address their ordinary problems to the village courts and to appeal unusual problems to the district court. They have sought a balance even in the use of different remedies for particular kinds of complaints. However, in examining court dockets, the anthropologist learns that with state law we have something new: the justice motive is often managed and controlled from a central station that is connected to state, national, and international politics.

New anthropological research in places like Papua New Guinea and Peru illustrates the widening horizon of the disputing processes. In Peru, as in the New Guinea case discussed earlier, indigenous law is having to deal directly with the nation-state and with corporations that are sometimes larger and richer than nation-states. In the Peruvian Amazon, the territorial rights to the indigenous land have become increasingly precarious (Urteaga-Crovetto 1999). Though the state has granted property titles to native communities, the state still owns the subsoil resources, and these lands are now under threat of occupation and misuse by transnational oil corporations, who, with the full cooperation of the state, are there to explore for and exploit hydrocarbon resources. Some communities acquiesce and assimilate to the bottom of the ladder. Others fight for real rights, with the aid of anthropologists and lawyers, by negotiating issues concerning the impact of development in their environment. There is disagreement as to what these contradictions between legal centralism and indigenous territorial rights mean to the local people. Again, local sovereignty connects indigenous causes with the international legal sphere to resolve the dilemma of claims that are absorbed by the regulatory practice of the state under the guise of national interests.

From the perspective of a traditional legal anthropology, all this makes it doubly interesting to read statements about the behavior of courts by United States scholars; the authors of these statements speak about courts as if they were persons. In one such article, Sam Krislov (1983) notes that courts can encourage court use by narrowing or broadening their understanding of who may litigate and can generate activity by rewarding lawyers, granting attorney's fees, and controlling the supply of lawyers. Accordingly, it is not the plaintiff but the court that is the dominant user and major player that determines whether litigation contracts or expands. Krislov further observes that litigation is also a product of social propensities to litigate, and the rate of litigation is often influenced by increases in the number of transactions and by the presence of outside alternatives. He rejects the popular notion that individual plaintiffs are the major actors in generating litigation in favor of the idea of "the Law gives," an idea that is "a recent entry into the domain of Law," as Professor Sacco notes (1995). If Krislov and others are correct in suggesting that the court itself controls the rate of court use, why, we might ask, is there so much concentrated activity in the 1990s directed to closing plaintiff access to civil litigation in the United States?

JUSTICE OR INJUSTICE?

The modern law of "civil wrongs" encompasses the law of torts. Probably 90 percent of all modern litigated tort cases fall under the rubric of personal injury (Friedman 1985). Lawrence Friedman argues that before the Industrial Revolution and the coming of modern machines, redress for bodily injury was difficult to obtain. He notes that in the first part of the nineteenth century, the law of torts grew in the direction of rules that put serious obstacles in the way of personal injury actions by workers, passengers, and pedestrians: "The rules favored defendants over plaintiffs, businesses over individuals" (54). As Friedman and other legal historians regularly point out, this was a period of enormous economic growth and expansion, a time in which there was as yet no large and organized industrial workforce to secure workers' rights. The legal framework included legal principles of liability, fault, negligence, and the "reasonable man" and put at a disadvantage persons who were injured in industrial accidents in factories, railroads, and mines. A servant employee who was injured on the job could not sue his or her employer—that is, if the employer was that abstract personage, the corporation.

Twentieth-century tort law, on the other hand, insists that those who are liable must accept responsibility. In making the contrast, Friedman attributes the shift to the growth of the insurance industry, which, by providing social insurance, ensured that an injury no longer meant financial ruin. Insurance made it possible for the plaintiff to expect compensation. Although compensatory awards are much exaggerated by the media, twentieth-century personal injury recoveries have tended to be large in comparison with those of the nineteenth century because, according to Friedman and others, compensation has been the central purpose of twentieth-century law. Insurance helped transform the law of torts, or, at least, insurance and tort doctrine interacted to create a shift toward compensation.

What is interesting about Friedman's discussion of tort, compensation, and insurance, a discussion littered with terms like "total justice" and "total redress," is the lack of a comparative or macrohistorical perspective that breaks away from the limits of traditional legal history to encompass an outsider's perspective. Anthropologists have learned that in most human societies, those who have been wronged, or who feel they have been wronged, expect compensation and believe that injury must stand redressed and that the wrongdoers must assume responsibility.[1] When legal scholars speak about tort law's move in the

---

1. Evans-Pritchard's monograph on the Nuer (1940) is a classic ethnography that examines wrongs in conjunction with compensation.

direction of compensation or a fiduciary legal order, they might well be speaking to the specific conditions that have arisen from industrialism and corporate capitalism.

Most likely, there will be a move toward compensatory practices, and as we learn more about the projected impacts of injuries caused, for example, by the Dalkon Shield, radioactive immersions (nuclear accidents, for example), and tobacco- and asbestos-related diseases, we see that damages can be both backward looking (addressed to suffering endured so far) and forward looking (addressed to projected sufferings). According to Friedman, victims "earn" compensation as a result of what happens to be a current social norm, the norm of total justice: "Law responds, unconsciously, to the climate of opinion around it": "new social norms. . .find their way into legal culture" (1985: 72). Interestingly, the general expectation of justice that he speaks of is not just American but most likely universal (Nader and Sursock 1986). Nevertheless, Friedman does not see legal culture's move toward total justice as bound to continue, and he acknowledges the possibility of a countertrend, presumably owing to changing *social* norms.

I could tell this story another way, and the difference in the telling is at the heart of the life of law, and at the heart of the naïveté in academic legal scholarship. The changes in law in the past two centuries did not just happen, nor did the law respond unconsciously. The changes came because of the cumulative sense of injustice generated by individual plaintiffs and plaintiffs' lawyers (among others) who argued cases or wrote legislation governing litigation. The movement in the law came from the experience of total injustice rather than from the demand for total justice and from rising expectations. As the jurist Edmond Cahn observed: "The response to a real or imagined instance of injustice is...alive with movement and warmth" (1949: 13). Justice is contemplative. Injustice is dynamic. A complaint about the production of Ford Pintos is about individuals being engulfed in flames owing to defective design, an injustice experienced in terms of the absence of remedy for the victim of the assault. The issue for consumers of industrial products is how to minimize industrial violence by transforming the structure and organization of the industrial corporation, with its limits on the freedom of internal dissent and its merciless focus on short-term profits. A sense of injustice may be the force that keeps industry creative and innovative. After all, how did we get seat belts and airbags? A sense of injustice also may be the force that, given its location in the intersection between the state and civil society, keeps the law alive. Thus, the goal of the plaintiff is not simply compensation but also deterrence (or prevention) and punishment for conscious wrongdoing.

Some readers may remember *The Buffalo Creek Disaster* (Stern 1976), a memoir about one of the worst disasters in coal-mining history. In February 1972, a massive coal-waste pile that was damming a stream in the mountains of West Virginia collapsed and unleashed more than 130 million gallons of water and black coal waste into the Buffalo Creek Valley below. More than 125 people died, mostly women and children. Many of the 4,000 surviving residents were injured, and many lost their homes. The author of the book and the lawyer for the plaintiffs, Gerald Stern, comments in his memoir that what made this coal-mining disaster unique was that this time it was not the male coal miners but mainly miners' wives and children who died unexpectedly that morning. In past disasters, the small settlements offered by coal companies were usually accepted, but this time a few hundred of the survivors banded together to sue the company, to make them pay, to make them admit their responsibility, and to make sure such an incident never happened again. The disaster was alive with the sense of injustice that Edmond Cahn wrote about. Stern reminds us that the legal system responded, and the plaintiffs won not only a settlement but "a new sense of their dignity and self-worth" (307). As one plaintiff put it, "The act of God (which the defendants had argued to these practicing Christians!) was when the people banded together for a right and just cause through the processes of law" (302). The survivors in the valley reacted violently to the company's attempt to blame God for this human-made disaster. But had they not been able to go to trial, it is anyone's guess as to whether there would have been a settlement of $13.5 million. It is probably also relevant that the pro bono lawyer in this case had been a civil rights activist and lawyer.

The terms we use shape the direction of our thoughts—justice philosophers or injustice specialists, rights specialists or wrongs specialists, departments of justice or departments of injustice. Perhaps we should say "injustice," for that concept is the life of the law. Indeed, injustice is at the heart of dissatisfaction with the law and must be recognized as the motor of change.

MANUFACTURING TRENDS AND COUNTERTRENDS

Complex litigation provides a forum for anthropologists to understand and explore law drift. In environmental civil and criminal cases, a broad category of user develops to include exposed families and communities. The corporations that manufacture human and environmental toxins, federal and state agencies, medical and epidemiology experts, scientific researchers, attorneys, juries, and judges become participants in the drift. The way in which environmental cases (civil and criminal) are litigated, the presentation of information, the arguments about causation and harm, the process of judicial management, and the case outcomes reflect and reveal how the numerous participants come to understand law. Through the legal process, a participant-user worldview can become dominant.

In *A Civil Action,* Jonathan Harr (1995) tells the now well-known story of the cluster of leukemia cases in the Woburn, Massachusetts, case. This case was not about total justice, nor was it solely about compensation. It was about a group of American families who saw their children die of cancer as a consequence of environmental pollution. It was about the persistence of one mother, whose youngest son was diagnosed with leukemia in 1976. She discovered that the incidence of leukemia in the area was eight times the national average and that there was a cluster of more than a dozen other children in the neighborhood who also had been stricken.

When this clustering of cases was called to the attention of the Centers for Disease Control and Prevention (CDC), the search for the cause of the leukemia began. As the story unfolds, the reader begins to appreciate how difficult it was (and is) for plaintiffs to recover damages in toxic tort cases brought against corporate interests. The plaintiffs had the burden of proving that the contaminants in the well water had caused the children's leukemia, a connection that had not yet been scientifically demonstrated. Most of Harr's description of this extended case centers on the lead lawyer, who enlisted experts in cancer epidemiology, hydrogeology, toxicology, geology, neurology, and more. Although the Environmental Protection Agency was on the scene and had already identified three companies as possible sources of contamination of the East Woburn aquifer, the basic scientific research was being carried out as the case was being argued. The story highlights issues of class, culture, power disparities, awakened communities, and the place of perseverance and performance in the lawyer and the civil plaintiffs who took on this mass toxic case in the first place against companies like W. R. Grace and Beatrice Foods. What originally looked like a medical problem became a public health problem and then a problem of law.

In 1979, two public wells that supplied drinking water to the area were found to be highly contaminated with toxic industrial solvents. The mother suspected a connection but could get no answers from public health officials. Eight families sued Grace and Beatrice, who stood accused of polluting the water supply in East Woburn and causing death and injury to the children. Their families' lawyer spent close to nine years and almost a million dollars of his own money on the case, and the jury ultimately found W. R. Grace, but not Beatrice Foods, negligent for dumping toxic waste. As in other mass tort trials, complexity became a problem.

The segmentation of the trial was part of the managerial judge's movement for economy and time-saving results; experts refer to this segmentation as polyfurcation, the separation of interwoven issues. Some argue that polyfurcation of trials in complex tort cases could infringe on the Seventh Amendment, which ensures a plaintiff's right to a jury trial: "Juries are forced by judicial and legal boundaries to hear only one part of the controversy and their ability to weigh links between the legal elements disappears" (Smith 1998). In the Woburn case, the judge trifurcated the trial; the link between Grace, Beatrice, and the water and the link between the water and the injuries were presented separately, which made it difficult for the jury to comprehend the link or to add fairness to the verdict. The judge's demands for "concluding evidence" and the defendants' legal maneuvers further complicated the case. The evidence amounted to a thousand pages of files that included medical proofs, scientific tests, public reports, depositions, and so on. The case was so complicated that the jury could not find the exact date of the contamination of the wells or any "concluding evidence" of the responsibility of Beatrice Foods. Three families were excluded from the case because the dates of the deaths of their children did not coincide with the random year the jury established as the time of contamination of the wells. The accusation against W. R. Grace was also at risk. Because the judge's ruling found no evidence to implicate Beatrice, the plaintiffs' lawyers were forced to negotiate with W. R. Grace. Initially some of the plaintiffs opposed any negotiation, but finally they agreed that a good settlement would stand for the corporation's public admission of guilt. Instead of a verdict declaring the corporations guilty of pollution, each family got half a million dollars. The settlement reflected the goals of an efficiency model.

Some time after the settlement, the Environmental Protection Agency concluded that "both Grace and Beatrice were responsible for contaminating the Aberjona aquifer and the city wells" (Harr 1995: 456). With this new evidence, the plaintiffs' lawyers attempted to appeal the verdict declaring Beatrice's lack of responsibility, but the judge's dismissal of the EPA report as concluding evidence blocked the appeal. In spite of these judicial artifices, scientific research since then has demonstrated an unequivocal link between industrial pollution and human disease. Yet on W. R. Grace's Web page on Woburn, the company continues to state, "We are confident that Grace did not contaminate Woburn's drinking water."[2] This assertion, after a decade of litigation, speaks to the company confidence in the power of repetition.

Harr's account goes beyond compensation to matters of deterrence and social responsibility and illustrates the pervasive ideological nature of extrajudicial complaint mechanisms sometimes propelled from within the judicial courtrooms. The judge in the Woburn case, who so strongly favored the final out-of-court settlement, went on to specialize in mediation after his retirement, as did one of plaintiffs' lawyers, Jan Schlichtmann, who confesses he is now a convert to negotiating toxic torts instead of litigating them. And a follow-up on this story reflects the need for an even wider angle of vision that includes government responsibility for protecting the public in the first place, a lesson that was imperfectly learned in Woburn, a lesson even less likely to be part of a case if confidential negotiating procedures are the primary remedy for complainants.

Controlling ideologies reinforce dominant players. The current trend in cases of community exposure to corporate pollution is to settle before litigation, to provide negotiated sums

2. W. R. Grace, "The Woburn Story" (2000).

quickly for lawyers and stricken families; this trend represents "a completely different approach to environmental law" (Cohen 1999: 76). This dispute resolution approach has been employed in two important environmental lawsuits. On Long Island, New York, residents are pursuing negotiations after claiming that the radiation leaks from Brookhaven National Laboratory have caused high rates of a rare and fatal childhood cancer—rhabdomyosarcoma. In Toms River, New Jersey, the same negotiation mode has been used to obtain a monetary settlement among Union Carbide, Ciba Specialty Chemicals, and the Toms River community, in which there have been more than one hundred cases of childhood cancer. Community members are negotiating with Carbide and Ciba rather than litigating. The corporations are settling but stating that they "see no evidence that the groundwater on this site is associated with the childhood cancers" (76). The result of such negotiated settlements, that the defendant settles without admitting liability, is that the defendant pays the money, cleans the site so that it meets minimum state standards, and then relocates. The corporation does not need to endure social responsibility for its conduct, and the "difficult" legal connections between the industrial and pesticide chemicals and cancer are often not tried, tested, or explored.

Controlling ideologies like those underpinning out-of-court negotiations are commonly employed by producers and serve as a means of control. Moreover, such ideologies decrease the use of court mechanisms by which consumers could win block solutions for complaints that seem to be preventable. In the cases cited, negotiation ideologies deflected product and service complaints in such a way as to benefit the business group. Out-of-court negotiations also reinforce the repeat players of the judicial system, thereby expelling the system's potential users (Nader 1989). Here, the drift of law moves with the dominant users, in this case, corporate users; and as Marc Galanter (1974) has taught us, the "haves" come out ahead. Yet there have been surprise factors.

Lawsuits over the harms caused by tobacco use bring to the fore dimensions different from those of the Woburn case because of the visibility and pervasiveness of smoking both in the United States and elsewhere. The story of tobacco is disjointed: we could go back in time to 1492, when Christopher Columbus encountered American Indians chewing aromatic leaves and smoking them in a pipe, and to the subsequent spread of tobacco, along with coffee, chocolate, and sugarcane, worldwide. Here, I limit the story to the various waves of anti-tobacco litigation and settlements that have been building in the United States since the 1950s, having been preceded by anti-tobacco movements since the nineteenth century. The number of books and articles on tobacco litigation just in the past ten years is immense, and I will select only three texts to discuss the motives of lawyers and their plaintiffs in the dozens of cases litigated, and the even greater number negotiated by attorneys general over the past decade. The literature on tobacco litigation alone encompasses stories of plaintiffs whose family members have died of lung cancer; plaintiffs themselves dying of lung cancer; lawyers crusading against the tobacco companies; purloined documents that provide evidence of tobacco executives' untruthful testimony; scientists who research possible connections between tobacco and cancer, as well as those who defend smoking as exercise of free will and the anti-smoking movement as authoritarian; and condemnations of the American military for encouraging the addiction of young servicemen, servicemen who later indicted tobacco companies directly for their part in causing teenagers to become addicted to cigarettes. The story culminates in the great tobacco cases of the 1990s, the verdicts, the settlements, and concerns about what this tobacco litigation has meant.

What struck me in all this literature was the public's sense of outrage—how it was built, by whom, and to what end besides money and power. In 1990, a Lexington, Mississippi, lawyer, Don Barrett, representing smoker Nathan Horton on a contingency fee, won his case against the industry, but his client was awarded no money (Pringle 1998). Horton was a self-employed carpenter who had begun smoking two packs a day when he served in the navy. American tobacco took the case seriously. So did Barrett, a southern populist, a traditional Republican, and a devout Methodist. His was not the usual public image of a personal-injury trial lawyer. He was a crusader: the Lord had given him the opportunity to fight the wrongdoings of the tobacco companies. He was later joined by two other similarly fervent lawyers: Mike Moore, Mississippi's attorney general, and Dick Scruggs, a country lawyer. Together they became the prime movers in bringing the tobacco representatives to the negotiating table in 1997. Mississippi became the first state in the union to sue the tobacco companies, using as a cause of action the need to recover monies the state had spent looking after victims of smoking-related diseases.

Meanwhile, in Minnesota, the tobacco trial of 1998 charged that the tobacco companies knew their product was dangerous to use and that they lied about it. Attorney General Hubert

Humphrey III and his litigator, Mike Ciresi, moved from charging cause of death to issues of deceit and denial about smoking and disease (Rybeck and Phelps 1998). While Moore followed a settlement strategy, Humphrey became the public health advocate. Early tobacco cases, filed between 1953 and 1973, had had trouble proving the link between smoking and disease. Between 1983 and 1992, lawsuits had had scientifically based arguments. Of 813 claims filed by plaintiffs against the industry, 23 had been tried in court. Of these, the industry had lost two, which were subsequently reversed on appeal. Industry had not paid damages, but many plaintiffs' attorneys, such as Jan Schlichtmann, had been bankrupted. After 1992, the case against big tobacco was hit by publicity. Whistle-blowers Jeffrey Wigand and Merrell Williams generated unfavorable publicity for cigarette manufacturers, while Stanton Glantz, a professor at the University of California at San Francisco (recipient of four thousand pages of damning documents stolen from tobacco companies), and the FDA, the White House, and Congress all entered the picture.

Humphrey and Blue Cross and Blue Shield of Minnesota filed their joint lawsuit in 1994, arguing illegal conduct on the part of the industry. At one point, Moore came up from Mississippi with a proposal. Moore and Scruggs were laying the groundwork for a national settlement proposal with all the cigarette manufacturers. Humphrey was opposed: it provided immunity to the industry from future lawsuits, limited punitive damages and preempted FDA regulation, and he considered the settlement cost too low. As negotiations with the industry continued, Humphrey called these negotiations "The Settlement Train" because they allowed lies and cover-ups to continue. The Minnesota trial, *State of Minnesota et al. v. Philip Morris, Inc., et al.* ended in the spring of 1998 in a settlement on the plaintiffs' terms, one that ultimately released a great deal of information on smoking and health.

Some forty states have sued the tobacco industry. The last document that came to my attention was *The Public Forum on the Proposed Tobacco Litigation Settlement,* which came out of a meeting conducted by the Judiciary Committee of the California State Senate on November 18, 1998 (California Legislature 1998). The chairman of that committee, Adam Schiff, opened the meeting as an opportunity for public comment on a proposed agreement to settle the state's lawsuits against the tobacco industry. The agreement had been announced only two days prior to the meeting, and the tobacco companies had imposed a "take-it or leave-it" deadline that limited any public review. California Attorney General Dan Lungren was one of eight attorneys general who negotiated the agreement. The California attorney general's office declined to participate in the forum or to attend. California was the thirty-seventh of the fifty states to file and had a very strong case against tobacco for years of false advertising, deceptive practices, and antitrust violations. Schiff pointed out that claims to recover the billions spent in treating smoking-related illnesses would be released by the settlement. He continued: "California should have been the 'proverbial 800 pound gorilla' at the negotiating table. Why has the attorney general yielded?" (California Legislature 1998: 14). Mississippi had sued and reached a $3.6 billion settlement in 1997, Florida had reached an $11.3 billion settlement in 1997, Texas had sued and in 1998 reached a $15.3 billion settlement, and Minnesota had filed in 1994 and reached a $6.6 billion settlement in 1998. Schiff went on to demonstrate what and how much was at stake in California litigation. He concluded: "Having failed at the national level, the tobacco industry decided to negotiate with eight states of its own choosing... counting on these eight states to persuade the rest of the country that the settlement is in the best interest of the public" (7).

The speakers that followed Schiff spelled out the many problems with the settlement that had been privately agreed upon. Many complained they had had to read the agreement off the Internet, that they had had section meetings; no one had the attachments. And there was general consensus that the agreement did not hold tobacco accountable, that there were loopholes in advertising and marketing provisions, that the state would end up subsidizing the tobacco companies, and that while the industry could no longer target children, young adults and college students were increasingly fair game. All in all the agreement was not enough to contain tobacco use and force industry compliance, and at the same time it excluded public health agencies from the agreement. The president of the California division of the American Cancer Society, Dr. Tom Fogel, a radiation oncologist, concluded, "I think it is fair to say that this is a raw deal for California" (California Legislature 1998: 27). A settlement after litigation (a public affair) is not the same as a secret, no-trial settlement. No wonder law professors like Owen Fiss (1984) have written against settlement. The tobacco industry is still in the driver's seat. The consequences of Woburn may be different.

The publication of Jonathan Harr's book in 1995 stimulated renewed media and academic coverage of the Woburn case. The question Why was the Woburn case a civil complaint? was asked. It could have been a criminal trial. But the state of Massachusetts did not prosecute anybody. In two recent Massachusetts cases, however, there were criminal charges (Alexander 1998). Consolidated Smelting and Refining Co. and its chief executive officer entered guilty pleas in the Massachusetts Superior Court in Worcester County (*BNA Daily Law Report,* November 25, 1997, A-8). The criminal act was exposure of company employees to lead dust and other hazardous chemicals. State environmental inspectors found that surfaces inside the company facility were covered with lead dust, and federal inspectors found the concentrations of airborne lead to be more than two hundred times the exposure limit permitted by the U.S. government. This case, the first of its kind in Massachusetts, sent a message to workers and employers about the changing boundaries between civil and criminal categories and about the benefits of criminal prosecution of corporations for reducing the likelihood of workplace deaths.

In another case, *Massachusetts v. Hersh,* yet another metals company was charged with assault and battery and accused of exposing workers to waste oil and three chemical solvents, two of which had previously been cited in the Woburn case. There have been a dozen or so such cases from Massachusetts and elsewhere (Mokhiber 1996), and the *Corporate Crime Reporter* (e.g., Oct. 13, 1997) continues to report a string of corporations and executives that have been prosecuted for workplace deaths in recent years. The examples include the 1977 case of a Massachusetts fireworks company convicted of killing three workers after an explosion in an overloaded warehouse and the case of Morton International and two supervisors who were to stand trial on charges of manslaughter in connection with the 1994 death of a worker who fell through a sixty-ton pile of salt and was buried alive. Prosecutors did not file charges like this decades ago. Yet such offenses have their origin in the common law, and asymmetrical power relations are commonly a defining feature of legal dynamics. More recently (July 10, 2000), the *Corporate Crime Reporter* headlined a New Hampshire–based chemical company that pled guilty in an environmental crime death case and was sentenced to five years' probation and ordered to pay $250,000 in restitution.

One of the most celebrated environmental criminal cases was heard in Brunswick, Georgia.[3] On January 15, 1999, the former managers and officers of LCP Chemicals-Georgia (a subsidiary of LCP Chemicals and Plastics, Inc.) were convicted in a U.S. district court on numerous counts including the illegal storage and disposal of hazardous waste and illegal discharges of mercury and chlorine in violation of the Clean Water Act, the Resource Conservation and Recovery Act, the Endangered Species Act, and the Superfund law. In July of that same year, a federal judge sentenced a former chief operating officer of the plant to forty-six months in prison and imposed a $20,000 fine, bringing to a close one of the largest environmental prosecutions in the EPA's history. Since 1994, cleanup at the site has cost $55 million, and an estimated $100 million for additional cleanup is required. Other company officials were also charged in this extended case, which perhaps should be seen as economic crime with an environmental impact.

Legal scholars ought to make greater use of wide-angled empirical research in understanding what motivates users of

3. *Georgia Environmental Law Letter* 1999.

law, or in understanding what does or does not change. Richard Johnston, who researches white-collar crime, points out that the current downturn in violent crime affords the opportunity to look more carefully at economic crime. He points out that the likelihood of an American's being victimized by a violent crime is minuscule compared to that of being victimized by a white-collar crime. Yet there is no public awareness, no cause to act. There are no plaintiffs! Johnston plaintively asks, "Why aren't folks calling their attorneys general or the Federal Trade Commission when they are victimized by economic crime? This is puzzling" ("Interview" 2000: 15). Why aren't attorneys general more proactive? The FBI publishes data on street crime yearly in its *Crime in the United States* report. It does not have a similar report on white-collar crime, although there are rumblings about developing an economic crime index.

THE ROLE OF THE MEDIA

To develop a "realistic" understanding of law that approximates what is out there, scholars must describe law as part of the social fabric and look at user behavior and the context in which it occurs. If we do not acknowledge the nature of the gap between rhetoric and empirical knowledge, how can we explain the problems encountered by analysts of nation-state law in trying to make sense of the law in everyday life? Trends are not just continuous, nor are legal traditions point-counterpoint. The law is part of everyday life, as are the users of law, and in the late twentieth and early twenty-first centuries, image is part of the process, a part that needs to be recognized.

There has been a serious effort among sociolegal researchers to assess quantitatively the impact of media coverage on product liability cases. One recent U.S. study titled "Newspaper Cov erage of Automotive Product Liability Verdicts" was initiated on the premise that "Beliefs about the world of tort litigation can...affect legal, social, political and economic outcomes" (Garber and Bower 1999: 93). The authors of this study were referring to the beliefs of citizens, attorneys, judges, juries, legislators, and business decision makers. What Garber and Bower found after they examined newspaper coverage for product liability verdicts involving automobile manufacturers between 1983 and 1996 might surprise most people: for the 259 verdicts for defendants, there were almost no articles in the press; whereas 92 verdicts for plaintiffs, 16 of which included punitive damages, were covered. The authors note "modestly" that their analysis appears to be cutting edge. There is not much research. They underscore repeatedly (see Daniels and Martin 1995) the lack of systematic data gathering about the life of the law that might accurately inform citizens, attorneys, and others about the frequency, nature, and outcomes of lawsuits. Media coverage tends to focus disproportionately on trials "where plaintiffs prevail and where jury awards are larger than is typical of the system in general" (Garber and Bower 1999: 120).

Civil justice "reform" (or what critics call "tort deform") in the United States has been neither a legal game nor a state-originated effort, although lawyers and state officials are implicated. The reform movement has been a disciplined one, well orchestrated with powerful images, or what people used to call propaganda. The refrains in the media are familiar because they are ubiquitous, like any advertisement—a litigation explosion, a liability crisis, an insurance crisis, huge jury awards. A civil justice system run amok is blamed for everything: competition in the global economy, loss of jobs and downsizing, lack of personal responsibility, and more.

In a book published by the American Bar Foundation, *Civil Juries and the Politics of Reform* (Daniels and Martin 1995), the authors subject to penetrating analysis the images of juries and civil justice that stimulate so-called tort reformers. Daniels and Martin argue that the politics of ideas, rather than the best available evidence, informs the rhetoric of reform and the stuff of image making. Their presentation of the most reliable empirical data on jury verdicts in medical negligence, product liability, and punitive damages cases from eighty-one United States jurisdictions refutes the notion of a litigation "explosion" and the sweeping generalization that juries are increasingly pro-plaintiff, generous, and anticorporate. Like Garber and Bower, Daniels and Martin, conclude with a complex picture fundamentally different from that presented in the newspaper accounts of civil justice. They put it carefully: "Most simply, the rhetoric of the reform movement is a weapon in a battle for the public mind....Ideas and images in the political realm are marketed just like products in the commercial realm; citizens, like consumers, are treated as a passive audience receiving messages about issues as the marketers define them" (1999: 3).

The rhetoric of civil justice "reformers" is marketed in this way, and we must understand the marketing process before we can demonstrate the gap between what academic researchers learn by empirical research and the reactionary claims: that the civil justice system is in crisis, that juries are to blame for the "litigation explosion," that the size of awards has increased substantially along with the frequency with which plaintiffs win.

Allegations about the limited competence of lay juries, about the jury bias against defendants and in favor of injured plaintiffs, about the threat to the American way of life, as in loss of business competitiveness—all are part of a causal argument to justify immediate "reform." Daniels and Martin (1995) seek to outline the difference between rhetoric and what the best evidence reveals empirically, and they cite researchers as saying that the reform effort is "built of little more than imagination created out of anecdotes and causal assertions" (17). They do not argue that the civil justice system has no problems, but they show that the manufactured "problems" do not square with the data. In other words, they ask, is the rhetoric sophistry or simply propaganda, advocacy for a particular worldview? Legal journalists sometimes do a better job at answering such questions than academic jurists, who do not want to be contaminated by speaking about propaganda. But the academics would be well advised to read good reporting before speaking about "social norms" so casually; doing so would remind academics of the importance of power differences among the various actors and about the role of intense influence.

Similarly, the litigation associated with the safety of silicone gel breast implants was keyed into questions of truth and consequence. As a *Nation* article noted (Pollett 1992), the FDA hearing on implants revealed that Corning, the largest manufacturer of the implants, had prevaricated and stonewalled for almost thirty years, and plastic surgeons had marketed the implants as a "cure" for "micromastia" (small breasts), a constructed disease if there ever was one. Again the story was not just about compensation, although that was an issue: rather, it was a battle about sex, beauty, fashion, women's bodies, and women's minds. It was (and is) about women's autonomy, autoimmune disorders, painful scarring, and obscured mammograms (Coco 1994).

The McDonald's coffee case is an additional example of how "social norms" are manufactured in an age of media and image making (R. Nader and Smith 1996: 266–73). Start any casual conversation with Americans or Europeans on tort reform and the McDonald's case will come up. People remember that an elderly woman bought a cup of coffee at a McDonald's drive-in and set the cup between her legs. When she drove away, the coffee spilled on her and caused third-degree burns. The woman sued McDonald's and received millions of dollars—so the story goes.

In fact, the car was not moving, but the woman did spill the boiling coffee on herself. The resulting burns required grafting, and she incurred more than $20,000 in medical fees, which she asked McDonald's to pay. She offered to settle for $22,000, and McDonald's refused. Her lawyer was hesitant to sue until he learned that between four hundred and five hundred complaints had already been lodged against McDonald's for serving hot coffee that scalded customers—complaints the corporation had ignored. The jury eventually found the plaintiff 20 percent negligent, but they found McDonald's 80 percent negligent because the chain had been unresponsive to consumer complaints. The conservative judge said the coffee, which was 190 degrees Fahrenheit in a Styrofoam cup, was too hot to drink. It was also 40 degrees hotter than the competition's coffee. The plaintiff received damages, which were substantially reduced by the judge to $640,000 from newspaper reports of $3 million, and then the case was concluded in private settlement.

Punitive damages are designed to make society safer by addressing issues of social justice. Compensatory damages address the question of individual justice. Punitive damages have an entirely different purpose: they are designed to deter and to punish the wrongdoer. To put the settlement in the McDonald's case in perspective, the damages were set at the level of just two days' profit from McDonald's coffee sales.

Some have argued that the punitive damages should go to the state, a policy that would of course ipso facto reduce lawyer incentives to take product defect cases and thus would restrict civil plaintiffs' access. At the moment, according to a Rand Corporation study, nine out of ten persons who are wronged in product defect cases do not file a claim or even consider seeking compensation. Legal scholars have repeatedly and convincingly noted that the problem is too few claims, not too many. Richard Abel made the argument regarding the tort crises more generally in an essay titled "The Crisis Is Injuries, Not Liability"; he argued that "asserting tort claims and helping others to do so is a vital civic duty" (1988: 40). "The failure of victims to claim erodes the norm against injuring others, allows anger and resentment to fester, leaves the most disadvantaged victims uncompensated and often impoverished, and tolerates— indeed encourages—dangerous behavior" (1988: 37).

The Rand research also explored why, if so many people do not claim, some do. In a nonwork setting, Rand found, people tend to blame themselves and therefore do not attribute fault to the manufacturer, but if the injury is a product-related work injury or, especially, the result of an auto accident, the victim is more likely to file a claim. However, even those who do pursue claims are unlikely to pursue to trial;

some 90 percent of medical malpractice cases close without going to trial.

The rhetoric is evocative, portraying powerful defendants as innocent victims of greedy lawyers, and there are other legal horror stories. Crises are invented by the manipulation and de-contextualization of hard data, such as those found in the Rand studies, and by the use of partial truths. The Daniels and Martin study mentioned earlier takes apart the rhetoric and the emotional hype—the movement to close civil plaintiffs' access—highlighting how little is generally known about claiming. Claims and lawsuits, they argue, are not the problem, merely the symptoms. The battle is a battle for the mind.

In another vein, some state judicial decisions are opening court access that had been closed by compulsory arbitration clauses related to employment. In 1998, the United States Supreme Court let stand a ruling that employers may not force employees to arbitrate job-related claims (*Wall Street Journal,* November 10, 1998). Various judges have argued that mandatory arbitration is unlawful but have approved of voluntary arbitration agreements. What the future holds is unclear, but the judicial position held on mandatory arbitration may be linked to debates over class action.

Traditional tort cases include class actions such as those dealing with assault and battery or multivehicle collisions caused by intentional or negligent conduct. Mass tort cases, such as the Agent Orange herbicide case, usually include a large number of victims. Mass toxic tort law is relatively recent in American law, and it has inspired new legislation regulating hazardous materials beginning in the 1970s at both the state and federal levels. An increase in prosecutions, along with the growing problem of industrial chemical contamination, has inspired industry representatives to lobby for certain legal privileges and protections, working with the anthropomorphic notion that chemicals have rights and should be therefore be assumed harmless until proved harmful; industry representatives also lobby for ADR, that is, for removing the "garbage cases" from the courts.

As indicated in discussions about access to law, the direction of law, for the moment at least, seems to be evolving in similar ways worldwide, although with different consequences in places where the social and cultural structures are different, where modernities are made local. In industrial states, most actual and potential disputes are between strangers; the true plaintiff becomes only secondarily important as access to courts decreases relative to population growth and need (Nader, *No Access,* 1980). Although many non-Western countries are at different points of the industrialization cycle, in highly evolved industrial countries, a struggle is occurring over the fact that most product and service claims involve people of greatly unequal power who do not belong together in any community in which indirect controls might deter illegal behavior. Production is centralized in large organizations, as is information, in the terms of purchase and in perceptions shaped through advertising. In pre-industrialized locales, even under conditions of unequal power, the underclass pursue their needs through law. In eighteenth-century Aleppo, Syria, Muslim women, although segregated, were wheeling and dealing in court in real estate cases, one of the more available avenues for investment used to improve their social standing (Marcus 1985). In a recent work, Susan Hirsch (1998) describes how Muslim women in Kenya, in spite of breaking community norms of silence for women, take their family complaints into the public arena, which is one way of organizing public opinion and destabilizing male authority. By means of court appearances, they contest the image of the persevering wife and the pronouncing husband. Courts are complex sites in patriarchal Islamic societies and often function as social justice beachheads for women litigants, who generally win their struggles for justice.

Mindie Lazarus-Black (1994) found more of this legal assertiveness in the West Indies. Her observations make one ponder the hubris of current "modernities." She writes, "In the English-speaking West Indies, law made slavery possible and yet provided a way out of that condition.. . .issues of law and justice were as crucial to slaves as they were to masters." Historians missed the significance of that point. "Slaves made a variety of courts integral to their lives." She continues, "Litigants help construct the law by supplying issues and aggressively pursuing claims" (171). She indicates that some views of law ignore the agency of laypeople in legal change by consigning them primarily to the role of supplicant. On the contrary, laypeople play a role in the construction of legal rules. The form and substance of the law is being constituted by disputes brought by litigants who made the courtroom an arena for defining social relations and capturing the public mind. In *Contested States,* Barbara Yngvesson also supports a direction of thought indicating that "complaint hearings are at the same time moments of reproduction and of disruption" (1994: 148). Her well-known case is that of Charlie, a person without social or material resources to control the law, who, when arrested and charged with exhibitionism, created disorder at the heart of order through his defiance and parody of professional behavior. Such instances are mostly excluded by those who see law as solely normative. The law is indeed "Janus-faced"; it may serve those who contest power as well as those who wield power. But at the same time, I recall those who remind us to resist exaggerating the agency of the powerless. Charlie was after all a defendant.

LAW AND GLOBALIZATION

The path of the subaltern plaintiff is not an easy one, and therefore he or she needs to be driven by a strong sense of injustice. For the analyst, it is easy for the abstract to prevail. When the function of law as power equalizer diminishes, the role of law in everyday life decreases; in the absence of enforcement, lawlessness prevails. Indeed, the absence of prosecution has encouraged an escalation of lawless behavior among those who capitalize on the inability of the justice system to handle individual claims and the general unwillingness to support the use of class action or preventative measures. That this situation is now covered with "political ideas" (propaganda) has only complicated the possibilities for otherwise re-imagining the situation. Possibilities become even more complicated to imagine because distinguished American law schools are complicitous, as is the general American public, in setting the boundaries of thinkable thoughts, as Chomsky calls them. In fact, law schools are the shrines of legal rhetoric "because they show the indeterminacy and manipulability of ideas and institutions that are central to liberalism" (Kennedy 1982: 43)—or to neoliberalism, we might add. Legal training is geared toward cultural homogeneity; it is reactive rather than proactive. In Kennedy's

words, "law schools are intensely political places" (54). In recit-
ing their legal lessons, law students reinforce the hegemonic
discourse. The challenge is straightforward, fundamental, and
not abstract. Can governments regulate powerful private interests? Remedy in the face of such a challenge is as complex as
the discourse outside of law and is made even more complex
by the Internet and recent globalization and transnational efforts at centralizing commerce.

Problems of governance and accountability in the global
economy pose different challenges for plaintiffs. For neoliberals,
"free trade" is the ruling metaphor in contemporary globalization, and the displacement of government functions onto supragovernmental institutions to the benefit of global economic
actors so that they can easily operate across borders is occurring
under the umbrella of neoliberal concepts of economic relations
very much in the American style. For critics, there are continuities between free trade and colonialism and development.
The entrance of postcolonial nations into GATT in the early
1960s was accompanied by a shift away from legalism and toward pragmatism. The sets of negotiations sponsored by GATT
show an increasing tendency to use the term "conciliation," a
term that is associated with a jockeying for power. In this scenario, an international class of negotiators and technocrats
shapes policy for an international class of corporations through
international trading arrangements and elusive use of undue
influence. The possibilities for individual or collective plaintiffs
in such a context may look bleak, but there may be a surprise
factor. Law may be "the destitute camp follower of the itinerant
armies of transnationalism" (Barber 1996: 225–26), but law is
nothing if its authority in the end does not derive from the

plaintiff. The life of the law is the civil plaintiff, in whose story resides the possibility of making intimate connections with daily life; but that connection is filtered by controlling ideologies that cast the plaintiff in a negative light and by a legal discourse that particularizes daily life by means of the case.

The CLS scholars analyzed legal ideology as discourse and rhetoric. However, the discourse outside the lawyer's office or the courts or in the textbooks has barely been touched by analysts. It is that outside discourse in particular that has had such a powerful impact on the law in relation to the civil plaintiff. This is where, for me, Rodolfo Sacco's notion of mute law enters. We all speak with ease of the industrial process, or even of the postmodern world that follows, but we barely mention the dominant institution of our time—the modern business corporation. We rarely use the term except in reference to the legal concept of the corporation. The word "business" scarcely appears in works such as the recent *Law in Everyday Life* (Sarat and Kearns 1995) or even *Civil Juries and the Politics of Reform* (Daniels and Martin 1995). Thus, it is not surprising that "political ideas" or propaganda is so eagerly believed by the public. It should be standard academic practice, certainly for anthropologists, to analyze the discourses in and around dominant institutions. There is much in the social science literature about the state, enough so that the state is a known quantity, just like law, about which one is also able to whip up a public response— but not so for the industrial and postindustrial corporation, whose invisibility is just beginning to be questioned.

"Corporate crime" and "corporate welfare" are invented phrases by means of which the corporation is being introduced to the public. Corporate practices, hitherto mute or unknown, are being publicly recognized by new civil society movements. It is not academics who are leading the way in introducing the corporation to the public through concepts like "corporate welfare"; instead it is plaintiffs and citizen groups like the ones who took to the streets of Seattle in the fall of 1999 and exploded into the public consciousness. We may say that the plaintiff is the life of law, but such a concept cannot be comprehended if the discourse of wrongdoing (in addition to the wronged) does not grab our attention. As it is, the representation of reality within legal discourse overlooks key "figures." The foundation of civil justice tort law should be located outside the law in the mass conditions of global and technological processes. We should work toward an ethnography that goes beyond courtroom interactive models to include what is at issue—the conjunctions of people and corporations, technological processes, and decisions of power that are embedded in history. Anthropological projects have been concerned with variation in law, but more importantly they have been concerned with a theory of description that centers on context locally and through time. It is this illumination through contextual description that has taken us beyond conventional notions of law as social regulation to a consideration of the often unintentional and unconscious way in which people engage in the making and remaking of law. In this sense, ours is a science of connections.

If the law is, as Oliver Wendell Holmes said, "one big anthropological document," it may be time for lawyers and anthropologists to come together over the larger processes of which only the minutiae reach the courtroom. Law develops within democratic society by its own vitality. When considered in this light, the Woburn case, the McDonald's case, asbestos class action suits, and tobacco cases will take on new meaning and new proportions, and the civil plaintiff's role will be appreciated as something more than presenting a dispute to be managed. The stakes are high, and the task is urgent for us all. The twenty-first century will be a century by necessity preoccupied with the problem of toxins and garbage—the residue of unpunished lawless behavior of the past centuries' actors. Trying to chart new directions will require a fresh understanding of law and its place in the civilizing effort, and the courage to enable citizen plaintiffs to reclaim the law for the common good.

Epilogue

One role of a robust civil society is to overcome both normative
and cultural blindness to human suffering. This raising of awareness
requires deliberative efforts to counteract the vulnerability of
previously excluded groups; lessening vulnerability in turn depends
on developing inclusive forms of decentralized participatory
democracy.

Richard Falk

The study of law as a process of control and a mode of discourse
has become more sophisticated with the varied use and abandonment of schools of thought. Today the possibilities for
greater understanding of the place and power of law are wide
open, the ground is laid, and the issues are staring us in the
face: the imposition of dichotomous Western categories that are
embedded in cultural practices, categories such as collective versus individual property, justice versus injustice, statism (the belief that rights are defined by texts, treatises, and the like) versus
universalism (the idea that values are of universal validity), as

well as conflicting arguments about how law contributes to dy-
namizing culture.[1] The talent is there both in anthropology and
in law, where legal scholarship has moved away from a purely
technical focus toward a mutually constituting interaction between law and social experience. While acknowledging that law
is used as a means to power and mobility, and as a means to
exert control over human and natural resources, anthropologists
also seek to examine the functions of law not directly related
to control—like freedom *from* want and freedom *to* fashion the
future. There are today numerous best-sellers that historicize
the divorce of the "natural" from the human; many of them
deal with "ownership" of information, of culture, of the genetic
code.[2] A commonwealth of "resistance" is emerging in which

---

1. John Borneman's (1997) book *Settling Accounts* is an example of a
new approach to analyzing demands for justice. After the fall of the Berlin
Wall, retributive justice was a form of officially recognizing injustice.
Borneman describes the prosecution of an important lawyer in a case of
retrospective criminalization. The indictment of Professor Dr. Vogel was
for extortion. The West Berlin court was concerned about whether Vogel
had committed extortion as defined under East German law. Vogel was
responsible for approving citizen petitions to leave East Germany. A concern with the nature of the citizen is part of Borneman's theoretical contribution.

2. Among the many challenging books on these topics are Vandana
Shiva, *Biopiracy: The Plunder of Nature and Knowledge* (1997); *Uncommon
Ground: Rethinking the Human Place in Nature* (1995), edited by William
Cronon; Daniel Berman and John O'Connor, *Who Owns the Sun?* (1996),
which, again, deals with "ownership"; Seth Shulman, *Owning the Future*
(1999), which is about the battles to control the new assets that make up
the heart of the new economy; and Daniel Quinn, *Ishmael* (1992), a book
deeply informed by anthropological findings.

the biggest battles will be over property rights, the anthropology of ownership, of nature, of commercialism.[3]

Law movements in the United States in the 1960s were proactive. People do not adapt passively to policies imposed upon them here or elsewhere, particularly when these legal changes affect their culture, their social dynamic, their livelihood, and consequently their own systems of justice. There are idioms in legal processes that extend beyond the politics of power and control, idioms that open windows onto defining social relationships, that define and redefine justice, that provide entertainment and drama, that create new science as well as new rights and remedies and institutions, and that define culture as property, itself an exercise of power reminding us that culture is a dynamic process.

In the intellectual property rights area, we are dealing with a Western law of copyrights, patents, trademarks, and trade secrets. But the interactions of Western law with radically different systems of law challenge a number of basic assumptions in Western law—for example, notions that one cannot patent old ideas in the service of the group rather than the individual. The search is on for new legal instruments when the old will not do. I refer here to the emerging international law of human

---

3. Kathleen Lowrey and Jessica Jerome, University of Chicago, organized a panel at the American Anthropology Association meeting in 1997 to promote a dialogue about understandings of cultural appropriation and commodification; previous discussion had privileged the economic aspects of the appropriation of indigenous knowledge and resources, but this panel also addressed exchanges, translations, and mistranslations of often dissimilar systems of meaning and structures of knowledge.

rights of indigenous peoples. All these legal developments are present in the work of new collaborators: an understanding of appropriation, the emergence of new hierarchies, configurations of indigenous self-consciousness and identity, movements for autonomy and self-determination, and, in addition, further privatization of what some feel is an already imperiled public domain. Secrecy means one thing to indigenous peoples, another to large conglomerates. In many of these issues, indigenous peoples are making claims about self-determination and control of material resources in the idiom of international substantive law.

One purpose of this epilogue is to indicate that what I have said about the links between civil litigation and democracy in the United States and in many of the small village democracies in which anthropologists have worked holds equally true on a global scale, although between local, national, and international spaces, the connections become more opaque. Hegemony is internalized domination, whereby control becomes normalized. The continuity of international legal principles and philosophy is countered today by the continuing formation of an international indigenous expression of the justice motive—with its own discourses confronting hegemonies. Looking at the justice motive on a world scale means examining the mechanisms by which specific national and international institutions help or hamper its expression. When the principal law users are powerful states or large corporations, law become hegemonic because these institutions command the major instruments of state and private propaganda. When the users are the little people, they do not speak from a position of dominance, but they can marshal arguments of morality and legitimacy in constructing their discourses, which in no sense should be viewed as utopian.

The history of legal evolution shows us that the justice motive is a powerful force in shaping the law, though not the only force. That is, there are empirical bases to claims that the law can be made to serve justice; without the justice motive there is no social legitimation of law.

Movements such as those for indigenous property rights or international human rights invite anthropological thinking to return to basic concepts in social theory; the word for "corporation" in French and German is "society"—distinguished from community or *communitas*. We need to rethink basic concepts to meet the challenges of evolving legal contexts in the twenty-first century. The point is not that society is, should be, or will be more just. Societies and culture can be understood only when we understand the justice/injustice motive as a driving force. Thus, a more specific purpose of this epilogue is to relate the book to a body of research that is presently housed separately in anthropology—human rights and indigenous rights advocacy—as a first step toward a new synthesis of globalization studies, international finance, critical studies of law and justice, and an anthropology of law that is theoretically more centrally configured.

One issue that challenges current legal contexts is the issue of cultural property, which is becoming ever more important and controversial. The cultural property issue is a useful indication of the coming of age of anthropologists. The context is no longer set by us and our informants. "Our" people are overrun by prospectors of various sorts, and we have had to meet the limits of our naïveté. Whether we are anthropologists of law or not, we are having to deal with the complexities of law. And just to be anthropologists today we may need to understand modern biology as applied to copyright law, in addition to the usual fare of social organization, culture, resistance, and so forth. Advocacy issues are being forced upon us by the people we have traditionally studied. In other words, we are having to become worldly, as did our nineteenth-century predecessors in dealing with imperialist and colonial governments.

Most people working on the issue of intellectual property do not come at it from the anthropology of law. One can see this at a glance in the list of contributors in Tom Greaves's *Intellectual Property for Indigenous Peoples: A Sourcebook* (1994). Apart from anthropologists, this list includes general counsels; botanical specialists; ethicists; specialists in conservation, forestry, and traditional medicine; and native peoples. The issues they raise touch on ownership, commercialism, nature, and what is patentable—subjects of general interest that attract a broad readership and an authorship informed by and overlapping with traditional anthropological issues, issues being raised by anthropologists who, as I have pointed out, might never have had an interest in law to begin with. For these practitioners, the route to this subject matter is otherwise: their route goes through human rights, indigenous rights, an interest in international networks of finance; all these subject matters contribute to the ability of ethnographers to understand the legal and commercial contexts that affect local communities.

To understand fully the contemporary issues about intellectual property, we need to look into history for the roots of Western concepts of individual ownership. Legal language is both a conceptual framework and a powerful practice that maps and expresses a social taking of the most tangible sort, for therein lie rights to land (Mertz 1988).[4] Nancy Williams's (1986) record of the Yolngu of Australia—a community of 1,000 people who were transformed into plaintiffs after the establishment of a mission station on their lands and the subsequent establishment of a large bauxite mine, processing plant, and town of 3,500 non-Aborigines–brought to bear the contemporary use of *The Law of Nations,* published in 1758 by Emer de Vattel, a Swiss philosopher and statesman. Vattel clothed the colonial appropriation of lands with moral authority: his argument was congenial to the colonizing nations of the eighteenth century. As he expressed it:

> The earth belongs to all mankind.....all men have a natural right to inhabit it.....all men have an equal right to things which have not yet come into the possession of anyone. When, therefore, a Nation finds a country uninhabited and without an owner, it may lawfully take possession of it. In connection with the discovery of the New World, it is asked whether a Nation may lawfully occupy any part of a vast territory in which are to be found only wandering tribes whose small number cannot populate the whole country. We have already pointed out...that these tribes cannot take more land than they have need of or can inhabit or cultivate. We have already said that the earth belongs to all mankind as a means of sustaining life.... Hence we are not departing from the intentions of nature when we restrict the savages within narrower bounds.
> (quoted in Williams 1986: 127–29)

4. In her work on the handling of social context in law school pedagogy, Mertz (1988) observes the role of abstract logic and the allocating of social context to the margins in U.S. law school classrooms.

As recently as 1971 in Australia, a Mr. Justice Blackburn used one of these "early principles" in deciding an aboriginal land complaint, thereby supporting the colonialist view:[5] "a principle which was a philosophical justification for the colonization of the territory of the less civilized peoples, that the whole earth was open to the industry and enterprise of the human race, which had the duty and the right to develop the earth's resources; the more advanced peoples were therefore justified in dispossessing if necessary, the less advanced" (Williams 1986: 127–28).

Another contemporary example shows the pitfalls of applying legal concepts worldwide, as if they were universal, without regard to the local context. Aboriginal customary marriages include practices that conflict with human rights provisions, as for instance the practice of infant betrothal. Diane Bell (1992: 349) has produced a nuanced analysis of how the conceptual division between individual and collective affects the rights of aboriginal women. When one focuses on the individual rights of one woman without noting that marriage is a process that establishes alliances between families and that such marriages have implications for landownership and ritual obligations, the woman loses the checks and balances that earlier worked to protect women. In addition, Bell notes that women experience the power of the state differently than men do, to women's disadvantage.

5. See also Geoff Clark's "Mediation of Native Title Applications: A New Structure and Role for Anthropologists and Lawyers" (1999) for more market-style advocacy for ADR-type forums.

This insistence that individual rights in the West are exclusive of collective rights is totally misleading, especially since the main form of property in the West is the corporation, which is a complex of collective and individual property rights disguised by the fiction of the "legal person." The focus on individual rights versus collective rights is critical for those indigenous peoples who believe that the group rights of Indian peoples are the most important and most endangered of all native peoples' rights. The right to self-government, the right to maintain communal ownership of land and resources, the right to preserve their culture, their spiritual life—all argue for a protected group human right. Richard Falk has argued that the neglect of indigenous peoples might be described as an area of "normative blindness," accompanying a modernization outlook that regards premodern culture as a form of backwardness to be overcome in the name of development for the sake of indigenous peoples (1992: 47–48). Their wealth in plant diversity and intellectual property is being stolen. Indigenous peoples' knowledge has been referred to as "the West's new 'frontier' in. . . 'the last great resource rush'" (*Cultural Survival Quarterly* 1991: 3). For centuries legal fictions have operated to secure the land of tribal peoples with rules of land tenure foreign to them. The same is happening now. Western ideas of individual inventiveness embedded in patents seem a bizarre mode of appropriation of the knowledge traditions of others, which is ironic because indigenous knowledge has for so long been scorned by the industrial world that now prospects for biologicals or molecular materials but is not limited to such. Entrepreneurs, or what Vandana Shiva (1997) calls "biopirates," are scouring the world.

For native peoples, the context is much wider: Intellectual property rights (IPR) are found in *Western* law—its courts, judges, lawyers. Many indigenous people are uncomfortable with the Western frame, but most countries are signatories to conventions and treaties that guard the ownership of intellectual property.

Culture, by custom and by law, could not be owned until recently. Now new owners of traditional knowledge established through law boundaries can exclude, and beyond that, prosecute those who would use the collective heritage of their own people by means of the WTO Agreement on TRIPs. The most famous case, mentioned earlier, is that of the neem tree (*Azadirachta indica*) of India, a large tree whose trunk, bark, fruit, and seeds have for centuries been used by the people of India for medicinal, fuel, and agricultural needs. Since 1985, more than thirty U.S. and Japanese firms have taken out patents on neem-based products. Indian activist scientists and farmers assert that multinationals have no right to appropriate the fruit of centuries of Indian research (Shiva 1996). Local users are now competing for neem seeds with transnational companies. Countries like India and Brazil have a tradition of not allowing patents on things clearly essential for life, but such countries are in the minority; the race to patent the planet continues.

Why is it that intellectual property law is often acknowledged as inappropriate for indigenous knowledge? How do these legal categories work? An example of how an anthropological perspective can shed light on issues of intellectual property is illustrated nicely by the Kayapo case in Brazil. Jessica Jerome has examined the language of GATT and the

TRIPs agreement in relation to the Kayapo of Brazil (1995: 1–48). Article 27 of the TRIPs agreement maintains that for an invention to be patented, it must be must be "non-obvious" (substantially altered from a natural state), useful, and novel, and it must be the product of a specific individual. Jerome writes that the Kayapo conception of what constitutes human invention differs radically from that defined by the TRIPs agreement definition. First, the Kayapo consider knowledge to be a product of nature and not of human nature. Second, Kayapo knowledge is not always translated into "useful products." The third criterion of the TRIPs agreement requires an invention not to have been known, yet indigenous knowledge is passed down from generation to generation. Any Kayapo can know a cure—it is in the public domain. The final criterion, that it be considered the product of a specific individual, would not square among the Kayapo, for their knowledge is communal and difficult to attribute to one particular person—unless perhaps the Kayapo were considered a corporation. Jerome concludes that intellectual property rights are not composed of values expressing the full range of human possibility but rather are composed of beliefs reflecting the interests of particular social groups and then universalized. The globalization of these particular cultural beliefs, however, serves to delegitimize certain forms of knowledge and innovation, such as the Kayapo's, and if widely successful such globalization may ultimately result in a backlash that would delegitimize international law itself.

Solutions to this ownership dilemma have been proposed: new legal concepts based on a more culturally inclusive depiction of intellectual property that recognizes the collective rights of indigenous people as "collective inventors." Others suggest the use of contracts between extractor and extractee. There has been an explosion of debates published on solutions to these issues (see, e.g., Brown 1998). But it is not my purpose here to examine solutions or to review the literature. Rather, we need to understand the means by which recent GATT "laws" have been legitimated and why commercial interests do not just take what they want, by persuasion or power, without inventing legal fictions and legal circumventions. Specific examples reveal a good deal about constructed conceptions of nature and humanity.

There is, as I mentioned earlier, a continuity in language. Since the seventeenth and eighteenth centuries, the same language has appeared and reappeared in new contexts. Jerome (1998) is one among several anthropologists who examine texts. Jerome analyzed two contemporary international legal documents: *The Convention on Biological Diversity,* a result of the 1992 United Nations Conference on Environment and Development, and *Trade-Related Aspects of Intellectual Property Rights,* the result of the round of GATT negotiations that ended in 1994 (at which time GATT was absorbed into the WTO). She asks What counts as "nature" at the close of the twentieth century? How do environmental agreements speak about nature? What kind of nature? To whom does it belong? And what do environmental agreements indicate about human-nature relations? The question of belonging is clear-cut: authority rests with national governments, although "the common heritage of mankind" appears and is a hotly contested north/south battle over national rights to prevent access to genetic resources while the interests of local and indigenous populations are disregarded. Jerome reports on the WTO's insistence on a role for biotechnology, a role that neglects the millennia of labor performed by traditional farmers and indigenous peoples in the breeding and conservation practices that nourished the biodiversity in the first place. The conservation of natural resources is treated as "raw nature," while laboratory nature is the manufacturer deserving of intellectual property protection.

The newest international intellectual property law has now overridden national systems of intellectual property protection. Jerome's work, along with that of others, points to the importance of recognizing the conscious reconstruction of legal categories (nature, in this instance) subjectively, selectively, and purposefully—such reconstruction is a mode of excluding the knowledge and resources of indigenous and other marginalized peoples from protection by law. Conceptual categories are indeed powerful.

It is extremely useful to take articles of conventions seriously.[6] As Kathleen Lowrey (1997) puts it, "Transnational indigenous political activism over issues of traditional knowledge appropriation is absolutely not a salvage operation by 'dying'

6. Annelise Riles studies the network of nongovernmental organizations (NGOs) in the Pacific, documents from United Nations conferences, and the world of international bureaucratic practices. In preparing for the Fourth World Conference for Women in Beijing, she notes that design precedes agreement, and practitioners are back to legal formalism: "The manufacture of desire through mundane 'technicalities'" (2000: 181). Also see Richard Wilson's *Human Rights, Culture, and Context* (1997). Wilson describes how rights-based discourses are used in different contexts as a way of articulating the tension between global and local formulations of human rights that are structured by transnational practices.

people, but instead indicative of the growth of new forms of self-consciousness." Her analysis of a patent conflict between the Izoceño, a Guarani-speaking group in Bolivia, and a government-funded ethnobotanical research project is persuasive. The Izoceño live in the ecologically unusual Gran Chaco, and in the 1990s, by means of World Bank debt-for-nature arrangements, the Bolivian government became interested in sponsoring biodiversity conservation efforts in partnership with the Izoceño. One initiative focused on traditional plant medicines, one of which was noted to have powerful antifungal properties. A university team from La Paz developed trials for an antifungal salve and proposed its production for commercial sale within Bolivia. Unfortunately, the overall project had the conflictful task of advancing "traditional knowledge" and commerce simultaneously. The patent would be held by university researchers along with the ministry of biodiversity conservation; royalties would not be paid to the Izoceño because the plant was traditionally used as a relief for stomach ailments, not as a topical antifungal. The Izoceño want to patent the salve in the collective name of the Izoceñan people, which would serve as model for traditional knowledge protection both within Bolivia and elsewhere. The case according to Lowrey illuminates the long-held fallacy that indigenous peoples are bound to disappear, and for their part the Izoceño have learned about the privileges of law, medicine, and science through their engagement with development as hegemonic imposition. Questions about law are now raised in a new environment. The experience appears to have been transformative. Newly acquired knowledge of the national and international world of law and economics in which the Izoceño found themselves as players changed identity politics and life's possibilities.

However, in a follow-up field story, Lowrey (pers. comm. 2000) describes another project, which she flatly states is not an example of biopiracy. Two Bolivian scientists, one an ethnobotanist, the other a biochemist, designed it as a countermodel to extractive ethnopharmaceutical research. They found funding to build a tiny laboratory in the village and trained a local shaman and two assistants in preparation of the salve, the idea being to produce locally and sell nationally, an idea that could bolster appreciation of local knowledge. Around 1997 or 1998, the project began coming apart. No one had anticipated that the Bolivian Ministry of Health would not approve the sale of this "medicine" without the supervision of a full-time pharmaceutical professional . A follow-up idea was to have a Bolivian pharmaceutical company buy semiprocessed extracts of the medicinal plant from the community, but that did not happen. The community was left embittered, the scientists disillusioned. Lowrey ends: "Small local actors are too weak to wield IP rights effectively and measures to limit knowledge-sharing will inevitably serve Goliaths instead of Davids."

Tom Greaves is more optimistic:

> What is needed is a *new legal instrument*—an instrument of the twenty-first century, that confers ownership and control of indigenous culture on those who practice it; an ownership and control that is society-wide rather than individual; that applies to what is already in the public domain; that, like ownership of property, confers an unending, monopoly ownership; and which is intended not to

ensure progress, but to better enable indigenous societies or village farmers to preserve and benefit from what is theirs. (1994: 9)

Others disagree. In the last two decades the biotechnology industry has won a series of legal victories expanding the scope of intellectual property laws.

Claims for intellectual property rights and profit royalties give rise to new categories for thinking about knowledge, material resources, and power differentials. These are highly complex claims, with histories that go back at the least to the nineteenth century and Alexander von Humboldt's New World journey to the lowlands of South America. Biopiracy is real. The issue of what is patentable is about who draws the line and where—in the courts or in the ministries of health. "The common heritage of mankind" is in fact mainly useful to the gene-deficient countries of the north. The stakes underlying the knowledge and power that are being constructed are addressed by numerous scholars who deal with boundaries, power, and knowledge (Nader 1996). But in the Brazilian instance, we are confronting the uses of law to reconstruct the category of nature for the benefit of particular social groups. International legal agreements are real; they have real force and systematically include and exclude knowledge. So, too, is philosophy real, as are the uses of specific conceptions of history set forth in theories of social evolution used today to justify commercial exploitation of native lands.[7]

7. Alex Geisinger (1999) analyzes the relationship between sustainable development—the driving force of international environmental law— and the spread of "free market democracy." He argues that sustainable

I should point out that tensions between individual and collective ownership exist not only for indigenous peoples but for U.S. citizens as well. We live in a period in which everything is for sale. Can we say for sure that we own our own bodies these days? Ask John Moore, the origin of U.S. patent number 4,438,032, otherwise known as the "Mo" cell line, whose case paved the way for the legal justification for the patenting of human material. In 1976 Moore learned that he had a rare form of cancer. When his cancerous spleen was removed, Moore's doctor discovered that the spleen contained blood cells that produce an unusual blood protein that might be used to develop an anticancer agent. Unbeknownst to Moore, the doctor, who was also a researcher at UCLA, began to grow a cell line with Moore's spleen cells. In 1983, UCLA filed a patent for a unique cell line, listing itself and others as inventors. By 1984, Moore had initiated litigation against his doctor, the regents of the University of California, and the pharmaceutical companies that licensed the "Mo" cell line, arguing that the doctor's actions represented a total invasion of his privacy and his right to control his own genetic code. The case *Moore v. Regents of the University of California* went all the way to the California Supreme Court, which ruled in 1990 that Moore's doctor had breached his fiduciary duty to his patient; nevertheless the court denied Moore's claim to ownership of the cells taken from his body in the name of medical progress. The counterargument

---

development is a force of ideological imperialism that eradicates ideas of nature held by other cultures. The implementation of sustainable development assumes the ability of science to develop technology to limit environmental damage while encouraging continued material expenditure.

posited that if human cells are to be sources of profit, the person from whom the cells are taken should have as much standing to own and profit from them as the physician and biotechnology company. Others thought commercialization of the human body should be prohibited by amending the Patent Act. Eventually John Moore negotiated a settlement with his former doctor, but a path had been broken for the ownership of nature (Annas 1993).

This recent work may indeed be described as law *and* anthropology et cetera, a burgeoning interdisciplinary field of people who are working on common issues related to basic research and advocacy in situations where "our" informants are active participants in driving the research agendas. Anthropology is political engagement, whether we want it to be or not. Such recognition liberates the imagination; context as an analytical device is not enough, nor is community. Schools of thought are blurred, and multiple mirrors combine to enlarge both the strategies of research and the recognition of common objectives, one of which is an understanding of the relationship of global to local as well as of locals to locals. Microlevel fragments and dislocations are now integrated with macrolevel questions that involve law but go beyond law. We live in a face-to-faceless world massively affected by global industrialization. In this world in which the complaint may be as important as the winning, the injured plaintiff keeps the law alive and reminds social scientists of the dynamics of culture. This observation can be read throughout in the ethnographies of the anthropologists and the texts of the lawyers.

BIBLIOGRAPHY

Abel, R. 1982. *The Politics of Informal Justice.* 2 Vols. New York: Academic Press.

———. 1987. "The Real Tort Crisis: Too Few Claims." *Ohio State Law Journal* 48 (2) :443–67.

———. 1988. "The Crisis Is Injuries, Not Liability." In *New Directions in Liability Law,* ed. W. Olson, 31–41. New York: The Academy of Political Science.

Alexander, S. 1998. "Getting Tough in Fight against Pollution." *Chicago Daily Law Bulletin* 144 (48): 6.

Annas, G. 1993. "Outrageous Fortune: Selling Other People's Cells." In *Standard of Care: The Law of American Bioethics,* 167–77. New York: Oxford University Press.

Attia, H. 1985. "Water Sharing Rights in the Jerid Oases of Tunisia." In *Property, Social Structure, and Law in the Modern Middle East,* ed. A. E. Mayer, 85–106. Albany: State University of New York Press.

Aubert, V. 1969. "Law as a Way of Resolving Conflicts: The Case of a Small Industrialized Society." In *Law in Culture and Society,* ed. L. Nader, 282–303. Chicago: Aldine Press.

Auerbach, J. S. 1983. *Justice without Law?* New York: Oxford University Press.

Avruch, K., and P. W. Black. 1996. "ADR, Palau, and the Contribution of Anthropology." In *Anthropological Contributions to Conflict Resolution,* ed. A. W. Wolfe and H. Yang, 47–63. Southern Anthropological Society Proceedings, no. 29. Athens: University of Georgia Press.

Barber, B. R. 1996. *Jihad vs. McWorld: How Globalism and Tribalism Are Reshaping the World.* New York: Ballantine Books.

Barnes, J. A. 1961. "Law as Politically Active: An Anthropological View." In *Studies in the Sociology of Law,* ed. G. Sawer, 167–96. Canberra: Australian National University.

Bateson, G. 1958. *Naven: A Survey of the Problems Suggested by a Composite Picture of the Culture of a New Guinea Tribe Drawn from Three Points of View.* Stanford: Stanford University Press.

Baumgartner, M. P. 1988. *The Moral Order of a Suburb.* New York: Oxford University Press.

Begum, K. 1988. *Tension over the Farakka Barrage: A Techno-Political Tangle in South Asia.* 1st Indian ed. Calcutta: K. P. Bagchi.

Bell, D. 1992. "Considering Gender: Are Human Rights for Women, Too? An Australian Case." In *Human Rights in Cross-Cultural Perspectives: A Quest for Consensus,* ed. A. A. An-Na'im, 339–62. Philadelphia: University of Pennsylvania Press.

Benda-Beckmann, F. von 1986. "Anthropology and Comparative Law." In *Anthropology of Law in the Netherlands: Essays on Legal Pluralism,* ed. K. von Benda-Beckmann and F. Strijbosch, 90–109. Dordrecht, Holland: Foris Publications.

———. 1997. "Citizens, Strangers, and Indigenous Peoples: Conceptual Politics and Legal Pluralism." *Law and Anthropology: International Yearbook for Legal Anthropology* 9:1–42.

Berman, D., and J. O'Connor. 1996. *Who Owns the Sun?* White Rivers Junction, Vt.: Chelsea Green Publishing Company.

Black, D. 1976. *The Behavior of Law.* New York: Academic Press.

Blackstone, Sir W. 1897. *Commentaries on the Laws of England.* St. Paul, Minn.: West Publishing Company.

Bohannan, P. J. 1957. *Justice and Judgement among the Tiv.* London: Oxford University Press for the International African Institute.

Borneman, J. 1997. *Settling Accounts: Violence, Justice, and Accountability in Postsocialist Europe.* Princeton, N.J.: Princeton University Press.

Brown, M. F. 1998. "Can Culture Be Copyrighted? *Current Anthropology* 39 (20): 193–222.

Cahn, E. 1949. *The Sense of Injustice.* Bloomington: Indiana University Press.

California Legislature. Senate. Committee on Judiciary. 1998. *Public Forum on the Proposed Tobacco Litigation Settlement.* Sacramento: Senate Publications.

Canter, R. 1978. "Dispute Settlement and Dispute Processing in Zambia: Individual Choice versus Societal Constraints." In *The Disputing Process: Law in Ten Societies,* ed. L. Nader and H. F. Todd, 247–80. New York: Columbia University Press.

Cappelletti, M. 1973. *Civil Procedure.* Tübingen: J. C. B. Mohr.

Carrizosa, P. 1989. "Making the Law Disappear." *California Lawyer* 9 (9): 64–67,

Chambliss, W. 1982. "Toward a Radical Criminology." In *The Politics of Law: A Progressive Critique,* ed. D. Kairys, 230–41. New York: Pantheon.

Chanock, M. 1985. *Law, Custom, and Social Order: The Colonial Experience in Malawi and Zambia.* Cambridge: Cambridge University Press.

Claeson, B. 1994. "The Privatization of Justice: An Ethnography of Control." In *Essays on Controlling Processes,* ed. L. Nader, 32–64.

Kroeber Anthropological Society Papers, no. 77. Berkeley, Calif.:
Kroeber Anthropological Society.

Clark, G. 1999. "Mediation of Native Title Applications: A New Structure and Role for Anthropologists and Lawyers." In *Connections in Native Title: Genealogies, Kinship, and Groups,* ed. J. D. Finlayson, B. Rigsby, and H. J. Bek, 141–63. Research Monograph no. 13. Canberra: Centre for Aboriginal Economic Policy Research, the Australian National University.

Coco, L. 1994. "Silicone Breast Implants in America: A Choice of the 'Official Breast'?" In *Essays on Controlling Processes,* ed. L. Nader, 103–32. Kroeber Anthropological Society Papers, no. 77. Berkeley, Calif.: Kroeber Anthropological Society.

Cohen, A. 1999. "Next Case." *Time Magazine,* January 18, p. 76.

Colby, G., with C. Dennett. 1995. *Thy Will Be Done—The Conquest of the Amazon: Nelson Rockefeller and Evangelism in the Age of Oil.* New York: Harper Collins.

Collier, J. F. 1973. *Law and Social Change in Zinacantan.* Stanford: Stanford University Press.

Colson, E. 1953. "Social Control and Vengeance in Plateau Tonga Society." *Africa* 23:199–212.

———. 1974. *Tradition and Contract: The Problems of Order.* Chicago: Aldine Press.

Comaroff, J., and J. Comaroff. 1991. *Of Revelation and Revolution: Christianity, Colonialism, and Consciousness in South Africa.* Chicago: University of Chicago Press.

Cronon, W., ed. 1995. *Uncommon Ground: Rethinking the Human Place in Nature.* New York: Norton.

Cultural Survival Quarterly. 1991. 15 (3): 3.

Dahrendorf, R. 1968. *Essays in the Theory of Society.* Stanford: Stanford University Press.

Daniels, S., and J. Martin. 1995. *Civil Juries and the Politics of Reform.* Evanston, Ill.: ABF and Northwestern University Press.

"Dealing with Obstructionist Leaders." 1998. *Peace Watch* 4 (5): 5.

Dellapenna, J. 1992. "Surface Water in the Iberian Peninsula: An Opportunity for Cooperation or a Source for Conflict." *Tennessee Law Review* 59 (4): 803–25.

Dezalay, Y., and B. Garth. 1996. *Dealing in Virtue: International Commercial Arbitration and the Construction of a Transnational Legal Order.* Chicago: University of Chicago Press.

Dill, F. 1981. "Law Reform and Social Inequality: Twentieth Century Revolution in Civil Justice?" *Contemporary Sociology* 10:745–47.

Dwyer, D. H. 1979. "Substance and Process: Reappraising the Premises of the Anthropology of Law." *Dialectical Anthropology* 4:309–20.

Ehrlich, E. 1936. *Fundamental Principles of the Sociology of Law.* Trans. W. E. Mell. Cambridge, Mass.: Harvard University Press.

Epstein, A. L., ed. 1974. *Contention and Dispute: Aspects of Law and Social Control in Melanesia.* Canberra: Australian National University Press.

Etienne, M., and E. Leacock, eds. 1980. *Women and Colonization: Anthropological Perspectives.* Brooklyn: J. F. Bergin.

Evans-Pritchard, E. E. 1940. *The Nuer: A Description of the Modes of Livelihood and Political Institutions of a Nilotic People.* Oxford: Clarendon Press.

Falk, R. 1992. "Cultural Foundations for the International Protection of Human Rights." In *Human Rights in Cross-Cultural Perspectives: A Quest for Consensus,* ed. A. A. An-Naʿim, 44–64. Philadelphia: University of Pennsylvania Press.

Favali, L., E. Grande, and M. Guadagni, eds. 1998. *New Law for New States: Politica del Diritto in Eritrea.* Turin: L'Harmattan/Italia.

Feaver, G. 1969. *From Status to Contract: A Biography of Sir Henry Maine, 1822–1888.* London: Longmans.

Felstiner, W., R. Abel, and A. Sarat. 1980/81. "The Emergence and Transformation of Disputes: Naming, Blaming, and Claiming." *Law and Society Review* 15:631–55.

Fisher, R, and W. Ury. 1981. *Getting to Yes: Negotiating Agreement without Giving In.* 2d ed. Edited by Bruce Patton. Boston: Houghton Mifflin.

Fiss, O. M. 1984. "Against Settlement." *Yale Law Journal* 93:1073.

Fitzpatrick, P. 1993."The Impossibility of Popular Justice." In *The Possibility of Popular Justice: A Case Study of Community Mediation in the United States,* ed. S. E. Merry and N. Milner, 453–74. Ann Arbor: University of Michigan Press.

Forer, N. 1979. "The Imposed Wardship of American Indian Tribes. A Case Study of the Prairie Band Potawatomi." In *The Imposition of Law,* ed. S. Burman and B. Harrell-Bond, 89–114. New York: Academic Press.

Franck, T. 1986. *Judging the World Court.* New York: Priority Press.

Friedman, L. 1985. *Total Justice.* New York: Russell Sage Foundation.

———. 1986. "The Law and Society Movement." *Stanford Law Review* 38 (3): 763–80.

Furner, M. 1975. *Advocacy and Objectivity: A Crisis in the Professionalization of American Social Science, 1985–1905.* Lexington: University Press of Kentucky.

Galanter, M. 1974. "Why the 'Haves' Come Out Ahead: Speculation on the Limits of Legal Change." *Law and Society Review* 9:95–160.

———. 1983. "Reading the Landscape of Disputes: What We Know and Don't Know (and Think We Know) about Our Allegedly Contentious and Litigious Society." *UCLA Law Review* 31:4–71.

———. 1986. "The Day after the Litigation Explosion." *Maryland Law Review* 46:3–39.

———. 1989. *Law and Society in Modern India.* New York: Oxford University Press.

———. 1993. "News from Nowhere: The Debased Debate on Civil Justice." *Denver University Law Review* 71 (1): 77–113.

Garber, S., and A. G. Bower. 1999. "Newspaper Coverage of Automotive Product Liability Verdicts." *Law and Society Review* 33 (1): 93–122.

Gardner, J. A. 1980. *Legal Imperialism: American Lawyers and Foreign Aid in Latin America.* Madison: University of Wisconsin Press.

Geisinger, Alex. 1999. "Sustainable Development and the Development of Nature: Spreading the Seed of the Western Ideology of Nature." *Boston College Environmental Affairs Law Review* 27 (1): 43–74.

Gellhorn, W. 1966. *When Americans Complain: Governmental Grievance Procedures.* Cambridge, Mass.: Harvard University Press.

Georgia Environmental Law Letter. 1999. February. M. Lee Smith Publishers and Printers.

Gluckman, M. 1955. *The Judicial Process among the Barotse of Northern Rhodesia.* Manchester: Manchester University Press.

Goleman, D. 1996. *Emotional Intelligence.* New York: Bantam Press.

Gong, G. 1984. *The Standard of "Civilization" in International Society.* Oxford: Clarendon Press.

Gordon, R. J., and M. J. Meggitt. 1985. *Law and Order in the New Guinea Highlands: Encounters with Enga.* Hanover: Published for University of Vermont by University Press of New England.

Gramsci, Antonio. 1971. *Selections from the Prison Notebooks of Antonio Gramsci.* New York: International Publishers.

Grande, E., ed. 1995. *Transplants, Innovation, and Legal Tradition in the Horn of Africa.* Turin: L'Harmattan/Italia.

Greaves, T., ed. 1994. *Intellectual Property for Indigenous Peoples: A Sourcebook.* Oklahoma City: Society for Applied Anthropology.

Green, M. J. 1975. *The Other Government: The Unseen Power of Washington Lawyers.* New York: Grossman/Viking Press.

Greenhouse, C. J. 1986. *Praying for Justice: Faith, Order, and Community in an American Town.* Ithaca: Cornell University Press.

Greenhouse, C. J., B. Yngvesson, and D. Engle. 1993. *Law and Community in Three American Towns.* Ithaca: Cornell University Press.

Griffiths, J. 1986. "What Is Legal Pluralism?" *Journal of Legal Pluralism and Unofficial Law* 24:1–55.

Grillo, T. 1991. "The Mediation Alternative: Process Dangers for Women." *Yale Law Journal* 100:1545–610.

Guevara-Gil, J. T., and J. Thome. 1992. "Notes on Legal Pluralism" *Beyond Law: Stories of Law and Social Change from Latin America and around the World* (published by ILSA, the Instituto Latinoamericano de Servicios Legales, Colombia) vol. 2, no. 5, "Struggles in the South," 75–102.

Gulliver, P. H. 1963. *Social Control in an African Society: A Study of the Arusha, Agricultural Masai of Northern Tanganyika.* Boston: Boston University Press.

———. 1979. *Disputes and Negotiations: A Cross-Cultural Perspective.* New York: Academic Press.

Hahm, P. C. 1969. "Religion and Law in Korea." In Kroeber Anthropological Society Papers, no. 41, 8–53. Berkeley, Calif.: Kroeber Anthropological Society.

Hamilton, W. 1943. "Review of the Cheyenne Way." *University of Chicago Law Review* 10 (January): 231–34.

Harr, J. 1995. *A Civil Action.* New York: Vintage Books.

Harrington, C. 1985. *Shadow Justice: The Ideology and Institutionalization of Alternatives to Court.* Contributions in Political Science, no. 133. Westport, Conn.: Greenwood Press.

———. 1993. "Community Organizing through Conflict Resolution." In *The Possibility of Popular Justice: A Case Study of Community Mediation in the United States,* ed. S. E. Merry and N. Milner, 401–33. Ann Arbor: University of Michigan Press.

Hayes, D. 1991. "The All-American Canal Lining Project." *Natural Resources Journal* 31 (4): 803–27.

Hertz, E. 1991. "The Chicago Syndrome." Unpublished manuscript.

Hirsch, S. F. 1998. *Pronouncing and Persevering: Gender and Male Discourse of Disputing in an African Islamic Court.* Chicago: University of Chicago Press.

Hoebel, E. A. 1969. "Keresan Pueblo Law." In *Law in Culture and Society,* ed. L. Nader, 92–116. Chicago: Aldine Press.

Hofrichter, R. 1987. *Neighborhood Justice in Capitalist Society: The Expansion of the Informal State.* Westport, Conn.: Greenwood Press.

Holleman, J. F. 1986. "Trouble-Cases and Trouble-less Cases in the Study of Customary Law and Legal Reform." In *Anthropology of Law in the Netherlands: Essays on Legal Pluralism,* ed. K. von Benda-Beckman and F. Strijbosch, 110–31. Dordrecht, Holland: Foris Publications.

Holmes, O. W. 1881. *The Common Law.* Boston: Little, Brown.

———. 1920. "Law in Science—Science in Law." In *Collected Legal Papers.* New York: Harcourt, Brace and Co.

Hull, N.E.H. 1997. *Roscoe Pound and Karl Llewellyn: Searching for an American Jurisprudence.* Chicago: University of Chicago Press.

Hunt, A. 1990. "Rights and Social Movements: Counter-Hegemonic Strategies." *Journal of Law and Society* 17 (3): 309–28.

Hurst, W. 1981. "The Functions of Courts in the United States, 1950–1980." *Law and Society Review* 15:401–72.

Hyndman, D. 1994. *Ancestral Rain Forests and the Mountain of Gold: Indigenous Peoples and Mining in New Guinea.* Boulder, Colo.: Westview Press.

Ikenberry, G. 1989. "Manufacturing Consensus: The Institutionalization of American Private Interests in the Tokyo Trade Round." *Comparative Politics* 21 (3): 289–306.

INI. 1992. *Perspectives for the Development of Indian Peoples of Mexico.* Caligrafica Digital: Mexico, D. F.

"Interview with Richard Johnston, Director, National White Collar Crime Center, Richmond, Virginia." 2000. *Corporate Crime Reporter,* July 10, pp. 9–15.

Jackson, J. H. 1989. *The World Trading System: Law and Policy of International Economic Relations.* Cambridge: MIT Press.

Jerome, J. 1995. "Intellectual Property Rights and Indigenous People? (An Examination of the General Agreement on Trade and Tariffs and the Kayapo)." Master's thesis, Department of Anthropology, University of Chicago.

———. 1998. "How International Legal Agreements Speak about Biodiversity." *Anthropology Today* 14 (2): 7–9.

Johns, G., and R. Brunton. 1999. *Reconciliation: What Does It Mean?* Institute of Public Affairs Backgrounder 11 (4).

Johnson, P. R., and S. F. Lintner. 1985. "Centralism and Pluralism: Legal Issues in Three Near Eastern Area Development Projects." In *Property, Social Structure, and Law in the Modern Middle East,* ed. A. E. Mayer, 237–62. Albany: State University of New York Press.

Kagan, R. 1981. *Lawsuits and Litigants in Castile, 1500–1700.* Chapel Hill: University of North Carolina Press.

Kairys, D., ed. 1982. *The Politics of Law: A Progressive Critique.* New York: Pantheon Books. 3d ed. New York: Basic Books, 1998.

Kennedy, D. 1982. "Legal Education as Training for Hierarchy." In *The Politics of Law: A Progressive Critique,* ed. D. Kairys, 40–61. New York: Pantheon Press.

Kleinman, A. 1999. "Moral Experience and Ethical Reflection: Can Ethnography Reconcile Them? A Quandary For the 'New Bioethics.'" *Bioethics and Beyond.* Special issue of *Daedalus* (fall): 69–97.

Koch, K. F. 1974. *War and Peace in Jalémó: The Management of Conflict in Highland New Guinea.* Cambridge, Mass.: Harvard University Press.

Krislov, S. 1983. "Theoretical Perspectives on Case Load Studies: A Critique." In *Empirical Theories about Courts,* ed. K. O. Boyum and L. Mather, 161–87. New York: Longmans.

Kroeber, A. L. 1917. *Zuni Kin and Clan, from Zuni Kin and Clan.* Anthropological Papers of the American Museum of Natural History, vol. 18, pt. 2, pp. 39–205.

Kuletz, V. 1998. *The Tainted Desert: Environmental and Social Ruin in the American West.* New York: Routledge.

Kuper, A. 1985. "Ancestors: Henry Maine and the Constitution of Primitive Society." *Historical Anthropology* 1:265–86.

Lambert, Craig. 1998. "The Emotional Path to Success." *Harvard Magazine,* Sept./Oct. ⟨http://www.harvardmagazine.com/issues/so98/so98issue.html⟩.

Laylin, J. G., and R. I. Bianchi. 1959. "The Role of Adjudication in International River Disputes: The Lake Lanoux Case." *American Journal of International Law* 53 (1): 30–49.

Lazarus-Black, M. 1994. "Slaves, Masters, and Magistrates: Law and the Politics of Resistance in the British Caribbean, 1736–1834." In *Contested States: Law, Hegemony, and Resistance,* ed. M. Lazarus-Black and S. F. Hirsch, 252–81. New York: Routledge.

Lazarus-Black, M., and S. F. Hirsch. 1994. *Contested States: Law, Hegemony, and Resistance.* New York: Routledge.

Lerner, M. J. 1975. "The Justice Motive in Social Behavior." *Journal of Social Issues* 31 (summer): 1–19.

———. 1980. *The Belief in a Just World: A Fundamental Delusion.* N.Y.: Plenum Press.

Lerner, M. J., and S. Lerner. 1981. *The Justice Motive in Social Behavior: Adapting to Times of Scarcity and Change.* New York: Plenum Press.

Leveau, R. 1985. "Public Property and Control of Property Rights: Their Effect on Social Structure in Morocco." In *Property, Social Structure, and Law in the Modern Middle East,* ed. A. E. Mayer, 61–84. Albany: State University of New York Press.

Levin, A. L., and R. R. Wheeler. 1979. *The Pound Conference: Perspectives on Justice in the Future.* Proceedings of the National Conference on the Causes of Popular Dissatisfaction with the Administration of Justice. St. Paul, Minn.: West Publishing Co.

Linnerooth, J. 1990. "The Danube River Basin: Negotiating Settlements to Transboundary Environmental Issues." *Natural Resources Journal* 30 (3): 629–60.

Llewellyn, K. N., and E. A. Hoebel. 1941. *The Cheyenne Way: Conflict and Case Law in Primitive Jurisprudence.* Norman: University of Oklahoma Press.

Lloyd's Economic Report. 1993. January, Año 27. Published for Lloyd Intermediation, S.A. de C.U. Investment Brokers.

Lowie, R. 1937. *The History of Ethnological Theory.* New York: Farrar & Rinehart.

Lowrey, K. 1997. "The Recruitment of Scientific Investigation to Creole and Indigenous 'Self-Fashioning' in South America." Paper presented to the American Anthropological Association meeting in Washington, D.C., November 19–23.

MacPherson v. Buick Motor Company. 217 N.Y. 382, 111 N.E. 1050 (1916).

Maine, Sir H. S. 1861. *Ancient Law, Its Connection with the Early History of Society and Its Relation to Modern Ideas.* London: John Murray. Boston: Beacon Press, 1963.

Malinowski, B. 1926. *Crime and Custom in Savage Society.* London: K. Paul, Trench, Trubner & Co.

———. 1942. "A New Instrument for the Interpretation of Law—Especially Primitive." *The Yale Law Journal* 51 (8): 1239–54.

Marcus, A. 1985. "Real Properties and Social Studies in the Premodern Middle East: A Case Study." *Property, Social Structure, and Law in the Modern Middle East,* ed. A. E. Mayer, 109–28. Albany: State University of New York Press, Albany.

Mattei, H. 1997. *Comparative Law and Economics.* Ann Arbor: University of Michigan Press.

Maurer, B. 1996. "From Caliban to Caricom: Encountering Legality in the Caribbean." *Law and Social Inquiry,* 21:1089–113.

Mauss, M. and M. H. Beuchat. 1906. "Les variations saisonnières des sociétés esquimaux; Etude de morphologie social." *Anné Sociologique* 9:39–132.

Mayer, A. E., ed. 1985. *Property, Social Structure, and Law in the Modern Middle East.* Albany: State University of New York Press.

McIntosh, I. 2000. "Giving Back the Bike: Reconciliation's Promise. A Review of 'Reconciliation: What Does It Mean?' by Gary Johns and Ron Brunton." *Cultural Survival Quarterly* (summer): 8–10.

Merry, S. E. 1988. "Legal Pluralism." *Law and Society Review* 22 (5): 869–96.

———. 1990. *Getting Justice and Getting Even.* Chicago: University of Chicago Press.

———. 2000. *Colonizing Hawaii: The Cultural Power of Law.* Princeton, N.J.: Princeton University Press.

Merry, S. E., and N. Milner, eds. 1993. *The Possibility of Popular Justice: A Case Study of Community Mediation in the United States.* Ann Arbor: University of Michigan Press.

Mertz, E. 1988. "The Uses of History: Language, Ideology, and Law in the United States and South Africa." *Law and Society Review* 22 (4): 661–85.

———. 1998. "Linguistic Constructions of Difference and History in the U.S. Law School Classroom." In *Democracy and Ethnography: Constructing Identities in Multicultural Liberal States,* ed. C. Greenhouse and R. Kheshti, 218–32. Albany: State University of New York Press.

Meschievitz, C. S., and M. A. Galanter. 1982. "In Search of Nyaya Panchayats: The Politics of a Moribund Institution." In *The Politics of Informal Justice,* ed. R. L. Abel, 2:47–80. New York: Academic Press.

Mokhiber, R. 1996. "Underworld, U.S.A." *These Times,* April, pp. 14–16.

Moore, S. F. 1986. *Social Facts and Fabrications: Customary Law on Kilimanjaro, 1880–1980.* New York: Columbia University Press.

Nader, L. 1964a. "Perspectives Gained from Fieldwork." In *Horizons of Anthropology,* ed. Sol Tax, 148–59. Chicago: Aldine Press.

———. 1964b. "Talea and Juquila: A Comparison of Zapotec Social Organization." *American Archaeology and Ethnology* 48 (3): 195–296.

———. 1965a. "The Anthropological Study of Law." *The Ethnography of Law,* ed. Laura Nader. Special issue of *American Anthropologist* 67 (December): 6.

————. 1965b. "Choices in Legal Procedure: Shia Moslem and Mexican Zapotec." *American Anthropologist* 67 (2): 394–99.

————. 1966. *To Make the Balance.* 16 mm, 33 min. Berkeley: University of California Extension Media Center.

————. 1969a. "Styles of Court Procedure: To Make the Balance." In *Law in Culture and Society,* ed. L. Nader, 69–91. Chicago: Aldine Press.

————. 1969b. "Up the Anthropologist: Perspectives Gained from Studying Up." In *Reinventing Anthropology,* ed. D. Hynes, 285–311. New York: Pantheon Press.

————. 1970. "From Anguish to Exultation." In *Women in the Field: Anthropological Experiences,* ed. P. Golde, 96–116. Chicago: Aldine Pub.

————. 1978. "The Direction of Law and the Development of Extra-Judicial Processes in Nation-State Societies." In *Cross-Examinations: Essays in Memory of Max Gluckman,* ed. P. Gulliver, 78–95. Leiden: E. J. Brill.

————. 1980. "The Vertical Slice: Hierarchies and Children." In *Hierarchy and Society: Anthropological Perspectives on Bureaucracy,* ed. G. Britain and R. Cohen, 31–43. Philadelphia: ISHI Press.

————. 1981. *Little Injustices: Laura Nader Looks at the Law.* 60 min. Boston, Mass.: The Public Broadcasting Associates. Videocassette.

————. 1984a. "The Recurrent Dialectic between Legality and Its Alternatives: The Limitations of Binary Thinking." *University of Pennsylvania Law Review* 132 (3): 621–45.

————. 1984b. "A User Theory of Law." *Southwestern Law Review* 38 (4): 951–63.

————. 1985. "A User Theory of Legal Change as Applied to Gender." In *The Nebraska Symposium on Motivation: The Law as a Behavioral Instrument,* 33:1–33.. Lincoln: University of Nebraska Press.

————. 1989. "The ADR Explosion: The Implications of Rhetoric in Legal Reform." In *Windsor Yearbook of Access to Justice,* 8:269–91. Windsor, Ontario: University of Windsor.

―――. 1990. *Harmony Ideology: Justice and Control in a Mountain Zapotec Village.* Stanford: Stanford University Press.

―――. 1993a. "Controlling Processes in the Practice of Law: Hierarchy and Pacification in the Movement to Re-Form Dispute Ideology." *Ohio State Journal on Dispute Resolution* 9 (1): 1–25.

―――. 1993b. "When Is Popular Justice Popular?" In *The Possibility of Popular Justice: A Case Study of Community Mediation in the United States,* ed. S. E. Merry and N. Milner, 435–51. Ann Arbor: University of Michigan Press.

―――. 1994. "Comparative Consciousness." In *Assessing Cultural Anthropology,* ed. R. Borofsky, 84–96. New York: McGraw Hill.

―――. 1995. "Civilization and Its Negotiators." In *Understanding Disputes,* ed. P. Caplan, 39–63. Oxford: Berg Publishers.

―――. 1997. "Controlling Processes: Tracing the Dynamic Components of Power." *Current Anthropology* 38 (5): 711–37.

―――. 1999. "The Globalization of Law: ADR as 'Soft' Technology." In *Proceedings of the 93rd Annual Meeting,* 1–9. Washington, D.C.: American Society of International Law.

―――. 2001. "Crime as a Category." *Windsor Yearbook of Access to Justice* vol. xix: 326–40. Special issue.

Nader, L., ed. 1980. *No Access to Law: Alternatives to the American Judicial System.* New York: Academic Press.

―――. 1994. *Essays on Controlling Processes.* Special issue, Kroeber Anthropological Society Papers, no. 77. Berkeley, Calif.: Kroeber Anthropological Society.

―――. 1996. *Essays on Controlling Processes, 1996.* Special issue, Kroeber Anthropological Society Papers, no. 80. Berkeley, Calif.: Kroeber Anthropological Society.

Nader, L., and D. Metzger. 1963. "Conflict Resolution in Two Mexican Communities." *American Anthropologist* 65 (3): 584–92.

Nader, L., and J. Ou. 1998. "Idealization and Power: Legality and Tradition." *New Directions in Native American Law.* Special issue of *Oklahoma City University Law Review* 23 (82): 13–42.

Nader, L., and A. Sursock. 1986. "Anthropology and Justice." In *Justice: Views from the Social Sciences,* ed. R. L. Cohen, 205–33. New York: Plenum Press.

Nader, L., and B. Yngvesson. 1974. "On Studying the Ethnography of Law and Its Consequences." In *Handbook of Social and Cultural Anthropology,* ed. J. Honigmann, 883–921. New York: Rand-McNally.

Nader, L., and H. Todd, eds. 1978. *The Disputing Process: Law in Ten Societies.* New York: Columbia University Press.

Nader, R. 1965. *Unsafe at Any Speed: The Designed-In Dangers of the American Automobile.* New York: Grossman Press.

Nader, R., and W. J. Smith. 1996. *No Contest: Corporate Lawyers and the Perversion of Justice in America.* New York: Random House.

Nelson, R. L. 1988. "Scholarship, Sociolegal Change: Lessons from Galanter and the 'Litigation Crisis.'" *Law and Society Review* 2 (5): 677–93.

Parnell, P. 1988. *Escalating Disputes: Social Participation and Change in the Oaxacan Highlands.* Tucson: University of Arizona Press.

Pollett, K. 1992. "Implants: Truth and Consequences." *The Nation,* March 16, 325, 329.

Posner, R. A. 1980. "A Theory of Primitive Society, with Special Reference to Law." *Journal of Law and Economics* 23 (1): 1–53.

Pospisil, L. 1958. "Social Change and Primitive Law: Consequences of a Papuan Legal Case." *American Anthropologist,* no. 60:832–37.
———. 1971. *Anthropology of Law: A Comparative Theory.* New York: Harper & Row.

Pound, R. 1933. "The Causes of Popular Dissatisfaction with the Administration of Justice." *Reports of the American Bar Association* 29: 295–417.

Pringle, P. 1988. *Cornered: Big Tobacco at the Bar of Justice.* New York: Henry Holt.

Quinn, D. 1992. *Ishmael.* New York: Bantam/Turner.

Radcliffe-Brown, A. R. 1933. "Law: Primitive; Social Sanctions." In

Encyclopedia of the Social Sciences, ed. Edwin R. A. Seligman, 202–6. New York: Macmillan.

Reay, M. 1974. "Changing Conventions of Dispute Settlement in Minjarea." In *Contentions and Dispute,* ed. A. L. Epstein, 198–239. Canberra: Australian National University Press.

Resek, C. 1960. *Lewis Henry Morgan, American Scholar.* Chicago: University of Chicago Press.

Ricard, R. 1966. *The Spiritual Conquest of Mexico: An Essay on the Apostolate and the Evangelizing Methods of the Mendicant Orders in New Spain, 1523–1572.* Trans. L. B. Simpson. Berkeley: University of California Press.

Riles, A. 1998. "Infinity within the Brackets." *American Ethnologist* 25 (3): 378–98.

———. 2000. *The Network Inside Out.* Ann Arbor: University of Michigan Press.

Rosaldo, R. 1989. *Culture and Truth: The Remaking of Social Analysis.* Boston: Beacon Press.

Rose, L. 1992. *The Politics of Harmony: Land Dispute Strategies in Swaziland.* Cambridge, Mass.: Cambridge University Press.

Rothschild, J. H. 1986. "Mediation as Social Control: A Study of Neighborhood Justice." Ph.D. diss., University of California, Berkeley.

Ruffini, J. 1978. "Disputing over Livestock in Sardinia." In *The Disputing Process: Law in Ten Societies,* ed. L. Nader and H. Todd, 209–46. New York: Columbia University Press.

Rybeck, D., and D. Phelps. 1998. *Smoked: The Inside Story of the Minnesota Tobacco Trial.* Minneapolis: MSP Books.

Sacco, R. 1995. "Mute Law." *American Journal of Comparative Law* 43 (3): 455–67.

Said, E. 1978. *Orientalism.* New York: Pantheon Books.

Santos, B. de Sousa. 1987. "Law: A Map of Misreading. Toward a Postmodern Conception of Law." *Journal of Law Society* 14 (3): 279–302.

———. 1995. *Toward a New Common Sense: Law, Science, and Politics in the Paradigmatic Transition*. New York: Routledge.

Sapir, E. 1921. *Language*. New York: Harcourt, Brace.

Sarat, A., and T. Kearns. 1995. *Law in Everyday Life*. Ann Arbor: University of Michigan Press.

Sassen, S. 1995. *Losing Control? Sovereignty in an Age of Globalization*. New York: Columbia University Press.

Sassoon, A. S. 1987. *Gramsci's Politics*. 2d ed. London: Hutchinson Education.

Schieffelin, E. L. 1981. "Evangelical Rhetoric and the Transformation of Traditional Culture in Papua New Guinea." *Comparative Studies in Society and History* 23 (1): 150–57.

Shiva, V. 1996. "Stealing Wisdom, Stealing Seeds: The Neem Tree of India Becomes a Symbol of Greed." *Gene Watch* 10 (23): 12–13.

———. 1997. *Biopiracy: The Plunder of Nature and Knowledge*. Boston: South End Press.

Shulman, S. 1999. *Owning the Future*. Boston: Houghton Mifflin.

Smith, S. A. 1998. "Comment: Polyfurcation and the Right to a Civil Jury Trial: Little Grace in the Woburn Case." *Boston College Environmental Affairs Law Review* 25 (3): 649–86.

Starr, J. O. 1978. *Dispute and Settlement in Rural Turkey: An Ethnography of Law*. Leiden: E. J. Brill.

———. 1989. "The 'Invention' of Early Legal Ideas: Sir Henry Maine and the Perspective Tutelage of Women." In *History and Power in the Study of Law: New Directions in Legal Anthropology,* ed. J. Starr and J. F. Collier, 345–68. Ithaca: Cornell University Press.

———. 1992. *Law as Metaphor: From Islamic Courts to the Palace of Justice*. Albany: State University of New York Press.

Starr, J. O., and B. Yngvesson. 1975. "Scarcity and Disputing: Zeroing In on Compromise Decisions." *American Ethnologist* 2 (3): 553–66.

Starr, J. O., and J. Collier, eds. 1989. *History and Power in the Study of Law*. Ithaca: Cornell University Press.

Stern, G. M. 1976. *The Buffalo Creek Disaster.* New York: Vintage Books.

Sumner, W. G. 1907. *Folkways.* Boston: Ginn & Company.

Tannen, D. 1998. *The Argument Culture.* New York: Random House.

Taylor, W. 1979. *Drinking, Homicide, and Rebellion in Colonial Mexican Villages.* Stanford: Stanford University Press.

Tomasic, R., and M. Feeley, eds. 1982. *Neighborhood Justice: Assessment of an Emerging Idea.* New York: Longman.

Trubek, D., Y. Dezalay, R. Buchanan, J. R. Davis. 1994. "Global Restructuring and the Law: Studies of the Internationalization of Legal Fields and the Creation of Transnational Arenas." *Case Western Reserve Law Review* 44 (2): 407–98.

Twining, W. L. 1973. *Karl Llewellyn and the Realist Movement.* London: Weidenfeld & Nicolson.

Urteaga-Crovetto, P. 1999. "Territorial Rights and Indigenous Law: An Alternative Approach." In *The Challenge of Diversity: Indigenous Peoples and Reform of the State in Latin America,* ed. W. Assies, G. Van der Haar, and A. Hoeckema, 275–92. Latin American Series. Amsterdam: Thela-Thesis.

Vidmar, N. 1992. "The Unfair Criticism of Medical Malpractice Juries." *Judicature* 76 (3): 118–24.

Wallach, L., and M. Forza. 1999. *The WTO: Five Years of Reasons to Resist Corporate Globalization.* New York: Seven Stories Press.

Wasserstein, B., and M. J. Green, eds. 1970. *With Justice for Some: An Indictment of the Law by Young Advocates.* Boston: Beacon Press.

Whiting, B. 1950. *Painte Sorcery.* New York: The Viking Fund.

Williams, Nancy M. 1986. *The Yolngu and Their Land: A System of Land Tenure and the Fight for Its Recognition.* Stanford: Stanford University Press.

———. 1987. *Two Laws: Managing Disputes in a Contemporary Aboriginal Community.* Canberra: Australian Institute for Aboriginal Studies.

Wilson, R. 1997. *Human Rights, Culture, and Context: Anthropological Perspectives.* Chicago: Pluto Press.

———. 2000. "Reconciliation and Revenge in Post-Apartheid South Africa: Rethinking Legal Pluralism and Human Rights." *Current Anthropology* 41 (1): 75–98.

Witty, C. 1980. *Mediation and Society: Conflict Management in Lebanon.* New York: Academic Press.

Wolf, E. 1982. *Europe and the People without History.* Berkeley: University of California Press.

W. R. Grace & Co. 2000. "The Woburn Story." July 20. ⟨http://63.111.43.6/Grace/Internet/html/woburn.html⟩ June 11, 2001.

Yngvesson, B. 1993a. *Virtuous Citizens, Disruptive Subjects: Order and Complaint in a New England Court.* New York: Routledge.

———. 1993b. "The Meaning of 'Community' in Community Mediation." In *The Possibility of Popular Justice: A Case Study of Community Mediation in the United States,* ed. S. E. Merry and N. Milner, 379–400. Ann Arbor: University of Michigan Press.

———. 1994. "'Kidstuff' and Complaint: Interpreting Resistance in a New England Court." In *Contested States: Law, Hegemony, and Resistance,* ed. M. Lazarus-Black and S. F. Hirsch, 138–50. New York: Routledge.

Zorn, J. G. 1990. "Lawyers, Anthropologists, and the Study of Law: Encounters in the New Guinea Highlands." *Law and Social Inquiry* 15 (2): 271–304.

INDEX

Abel, Richard, 203

Aborigines, 129–30; and Justice Blackburn, 200

Adjudication, 156

ADR (Alternative Dispute Resolution), 140–59; American, 124, 150–51; antilegal, 53; and Christianity, 129; and divorce disputes, 147; explosion, 146; facts and fictions of, 142–43; as hegemony, 56; internationalization of, 53, 149–59; language and rhetoric, 52, 140; mandatory, 146, 204; and Native Americans, 58; overhaul of U.S. judicial system, 14, 164; as pacification, 54, 141, 144; promotion by industry, 205; promotion by judges, 172; plaintiffs as patients, 141; supra-governmental, 14; therapeutic, 145, 148. *See also* Harmony law model; International river disputes; Pound conference

Advocacy, 218

Africa 121, 123; customary law, 1, 34, 53, 60; Horn of, 100, 133; indirect rule, 59; North Africa, 62

Agriculture, 64–65

Algeria, 62–63

Algonkin, 88

Alienation, means of, 44

Alternative dispute resolution. *See* ADR

American Bar Association, 47, 53, 143

American Indians. *See* Native Americans

Jurisprudence, 87. *See also* Fuller, Lon; Maine, Henry

Justice, 97, 182–83; access to, 45, 137–38; civil, 138, 200, 201; contemplative, 184; economic barriers, 109; informal, 105, 138; and law, 103; search for, 14, 169

Justice motive, 15, 44, 51, 164, 170, 179, 216, 217

Kagan, Richard, 34, 132, 171
Kairys, David, 28, 103
Kayapo, 222–23
Kennedy, Duncan, 207–8
Kenya, 205
Keresan Pueblo law, 92, 95
Kleinman, Arthur, 70
Koch, Klaus-Friedrich, 39n.2, 50
Krislov, Sam, 180–81
Kroeber, A. L., 25
Kuletz, Valerie, 125n.4
Kuper, Adam, 83

Langdell, Christopher Columbus, 89–90

Language: and ADR, 52, 140; continuities in law texts, 224; rhetoric, 49, 201

Lapham, Robert J., 64–65

Law, 2, 11, 63, 74, 111; access to, 15, 43–44, 48, 165, 177, 205; as agent of change, 10, 61–63; Anglo-American, 99; antilaw, 139; as antithetical to justice, 103; and boundaries, 28, 85–86; centrality of, 68; as constructed, 66; customary, 26, 37, 56, 89; definitions, 85; diffusion of ideas, 31; directionality, 13, 49, 98, 171; dynamics of, 50, 97; as embedded, 27; ethnographic study of, 20;

ethnohistorical models, 67; and everyday life, 102; evolution of, 35; history making, 71; and ideology, 118; indigenous, 4; informal systems of, 37; innovation, 96; international, 54; judge-determined, 173; legitimacy of, 17, 208; as means of pacification, 29; multiple jurisdictions, 117; natural, 99; political economy of, 28, 117–67; politics of, 102; privatization, 139; public/private categories, 87, 179; as reactive, 38; and religion, 130; theory of, 98–99; transmission of ideas, 118; universal, 9, 26, 86, 90; value-laden legal models, 13; Western, 214. *See also* Legal pluralism; Uses of law

Law and Modernization Program, 105

Law and Society Association, 10, 102, 104 109, 112

Law in economics, 10, 106, 112

The Law of Nations, 219

Law reform, 171. *See also* ADR; Pound conference; Torts

Lawyers, 63–64, 71, 142

Lawyers and anthropologists, 1–2, 9, 72–75, 115, 230

Laylin, J. G., 154, 158

Lazarus-Black, Mindie, 206

LCP Chemicals-Georgia, 197

Leacock, Eleanor, 84

Lebanon, 21, 36–39, 157

Legal categories, 8, 25, 225

Legal centralism, 133–35, 180

Legal concepts, new, 223

Legal drift, 170, 185. *See also* Law; User theory of law

Legal history, 69

Compositor: Binghamton Valley Composition
Text: 11/15 Granjon
Display: Granjon